chicago
unzipped.

'05
'06

chicago unzipped.

Publisher, Founder
  Benjamin Levy
Editor-in-Chief
  Julie Bartoszek
Head of Design
  Vani Oza
North Editor
  Kim Weisensee
Near North Editor
  Kate Puhala
Loop Editor
  Sara Campbell

Researchers-Writers
  Megan Brown, Lizzie Carlson, Lance Craig, Kristin Egan, Shai Feldman, Caitlin Grogan, Anika Gupta, Amanda Junker, Jeff Lee, Margaret Matray, Samantha Nelson, Brittaney Nicolas, Dayne Puhala, Brian Sabin, Kurt Soller, Brandyn Streeter, Frank Vu

Designers
  Ilya Bunimovich, Brittany Bekas, Kristen Dew, Elizabeth Polans, Neel Shah

Photographers
  Jane Lim, Vani Oza, Anna Patel, Olivia Tang

Contributors
  Adam Amaro, Peter Bartoszek, Andrea Bartz, Daniella Cheslow, Kristen Dew, Dustin Fox, Samantha Frank, Jen Howell, Molly Lipsitz, Haiwen Lu, Margaret Matray, Debbie Meron, Amanda Palleschi, Marcus Ricci, Stephen Ryan, Brian Sabin, David Simons, Salil Tamhane, Ilya Trakhtenberg, David Vognar, Ben Woo

Copyright © 2005 by NUCorp. 1801 Maple Ave, Evanston, IL 60208.

No part of this book may be reproduced in any form or by any means, electronic or mechanical, including photocopying, recording, or any information storage and retrieval system now known or to be invented, without permission in writing from NUCorp.

For sales or advertising information, email chicagounzipped@gmail.com, or visit http://www.chicagounzipped.com.

Chicago "L" map reproduced with the permission of the Chicago Transit Authority.
Photos Courtesy of: Adobe Grill, Billy Goat Tavern, Metropolis Coffee, Rockit Bar and Grill

Printed in Canada, Westcan Printing Group LTD.

to unzip chicago.

After six months of explaining our guidebook to inquiring friends, family and the management of the establishments we harassed for research, one would think writing the introduction would be the easy part. While our basic spiel is simple (a book for students written by students), actually conveying what you are about to read is a complex and slightly daunting task, as was the beginning of this project.

Dividing to conquer, we broke the city into three areas, North, Near North and the Loop, and those areas into neighborhoods. Part of Chicago's warmth is its composition of neighborhoods, each with its own identity and charm, as you'll read in the individual introductions. But how can a small group of college students have any authority to tell you where to go and what to do? Really, we can't, and this whole book is simply comprised of places where we had fun. Quite a few of us hail from other states and our center of operation was Evanston, and while this may seem a handicap, this assures you that the places are worth finding. This guidebook is the product of our discovery of Chicago, the souvenir of many days spent scouring city streets, the evidence of our exploration of the concrete jungle. Perhaps this is not a guidebook at all, but really a sappy romance novel. We fell in love with Chicago and we want to share it with you in a way to make you love every minute of it too.

Underrated author and Chicagoan Nelson Algren put it best in saying, "Loving Chicago is like loving a woman with a broken nose. You may find a lovelier lovely, but never a lovely so real." While the comedy club savors the irony of its name, Chicago is not a "Second City" because there is no city that can compare. Look into Chicago's history or even in the newspapers today, and you'll see the corruption that fuels Al Capone's legend. See and smell the remnants of the meat packing industry and remember Upton Sinclair's Chicago from your middle school reading list. Venture too far west from the glitter of the lake reflected off skyscrapers and you'll see Chicago's broken nose. But without losses, would Chicago's sports loyalties be so fierce? Without a history of corruption, would flourishing among Rust Belt cities be so sweet? Just as Chicago's winters make the summers more savored in memory's contrast so do the city's quirks heighten the experience of becoming a citizen of Chicago. Eat your deep dish pizza, shop on Michigan Avenue, but when you are ready to really love Chicago, take a closer look, and unzip the town.

to find.

evanston 6

lincoln park 54

loop 106

rogers park 14

bucktown & wicker park 68

goldcoast & streeterville 118

uptown 28

lakeview 38

oldtown 82

river north 92

index 132

Evanston

to eat:
Koi, Rollin to Go, Joy Yee's

to shop:
Fashion Tomato, Urban Outfitters, Fish Bowl

to play:
Century Theater, 1800 Club, the view of the city from the lake

Unzipped

Not far from home...

Often seen as the life of the North Shore, Evanston offers an eclectic variety of shops, restaurants, bars and cafes. Unlike most towns near a college campus, downtown Evanston doesn't live and breathe the average college student. Sure, there's the standard cheap fast-food venue or the popular clothing store around the corner, but Evanston also caters to a more contemporary and cultured crowd.

Founded back in 1857, actually due to persistent demands from the previously founded Northwestern University, Evanston has always been an adult oriented town that took advantage of the growth of the universities within the town. With the town right on the lakefront, Evanston's gorgeous outdoor scenery and popular (at least for the easy-to-please college student) night-life spots makes it a town worth a glance. While the more sophisticated crowd, usually with fat wallets, fairs better in Evanston, there's always at least one place to call your own in this rather diverse town. The Cultural Arts Center helps budding artists in the area display their works.

Not far away is the infamous Keg, the most popular destination for college students with nothing better to do than drink cheap beer. Evanston as a whole keeps the squeaky-clean image of the North Shore, but also adds the twist of the Loop with sometimes wild nightlife.

www.ChicagoUnzipped.com

to eat.

r Dogs, Gazpacho, Red Snapper, Pesto Mayo, Blue Ricepaper, Sheila's Dream Bar, Bake

evanston.

Rollin on your tastebuds: Sandwiches that always hit the spot at Rollin to Go. Totally worth stopping by before the early 8 p.m. closing time. Don't forget to try the bread and secret dip when you enter in. **910 Noyes St**, (847) 332.1000, **Noyes**

Tapas Barcelona

If you're the sort that likes tasting everyone's food, try Tapas Barcelona where sharing is the norm. The noisy, candlelit atmosphere makes it a great place for dates or big parties. You can enjoy a glass of sangria or amontillado and sample Spanish appetizers (tapas), like baked goat cheese and skewered beef tenderloin. You'll impress the waiters if you can properly pronounce the menu items but you don't have to practice your Spanish before going.

 1615 Chicago
(847) 866.9900
Davis

Davis Street Fish Market

Live fish tanks and crabs mounted on the walls gives Davis Street Fish Market a fisherman's wharf feel with a southern kitchen flavor. You can dine on fried seafood and gumbo spiced soups, slurp raw Canadian oysters and pick a cut of fish so fresh they sell it by the pound in front and finish with a slice of Key Lime pie. It's a mostly older crowd with the high price making it a good place to go when the family's in town.

 501 Davis
(847) 869.3474
Davis

Mustard's Last Stand

Looking for the full sporting event experience without paying concession stand prices? Stop by. Just a few blocks away from Northwestern's Ryan Field, you can grab a hot dog and fries to go or sit at the counter. Sports fan or not, being surrounded by obscure and classic sports photos will definitely hype you up. Even during the off season the place is great for a lunch break or even a quick snack.

 1613 Central
(847) 864.2700
Central

Sashimi Sashimi

If you think you like sushi, try Sashimi Sashimi and enjoy some of the freshest fish in Evanston. The place is ideal for quick take-out, with everything ordered on a checklist at the bar. Whether you order rolls, soup or sushi by the piece, the prices are fairly reasonable. The dine-in experience is a little mixed, with specialty eel and shrimp tempura rolls beautifully presented alongside miso soup served in Styrofoam cups.

 640 Church
(847) 475.7274
Davis

Koi

If you think that Chinese food is something that comes out of a delivery box

8 Evanston

Evanston

...rystone Clams. ... A Wreck, The Verde, Bocadillos

you owe it to yourself to try Koi. While their specialty Kung Pao entrée is fairly standard, the meals are presented artistically with a wide menu of Japanese appetizers that mix raw fish, sauces, vegetables and caviar for a swirl of color and flavor. Enjoy a glass of wine or green tea that steeps on the table while you eat.

624 Davis
(847) 866.6969
Davis

Dave's Italian Kitchen

Dave's Italian Kitchen is your typical family Italian restaurant complete with checkered table cloths and the pervasive smell of meatballs. It's a popular destination for Evanston parents with kids, so don't expect a quiet meal. Everything about the food is big, from the heaping cuts of chicken parmesan to the huge scallops and plump shrimp served with pasta in alfredo sauce. The real highlight are the homemade desserts. A huge slice of their creamy tiramisu will disappear surprisingly fast.

1635 Chicago
(847) 864.6000
Davis

Annam Cafe

While you might miss it from the street, Annam Café is worth looking for. You may be the only person eating there, but the food is high quality for the price. If you're hesistant to try Vietnamese food, just know Chinese food is similar. There are countless interesting spices and combinations, including duck served with colorful peppers; oranges and pears; and the Annam platter, a mix of sweet and spicy skewered meat, fried shrimp with mint, and crispy vegetarian spring rolls.

724 Clark
(847) 492.0631
Davis

Dixie Kitchen and Bait Shop

At Dixie Kitchen you can get a great Southern experience without the accents. The place is laid out like a country house, including fake windows, a tin roof and a stuffed raccoon with a fiddle. Try the cornbread pancakes and move on to the spicy jambalaya or gumbo, with a slice of pecan pie for dessert. The crowd

Evanston 9

varies, with college students packing in wings and $2 beers on Thursdays and families coming in Sundays for the fried chicken special.

825 Church
(847) 733.9030
Davis

Café Express

The walls are cream brick stucco and the air smells of coffee grinds and homemade sweets. Overhear the owner talking to her staff and you will have a catalog of Starbucks jokes to last you a year. This café is hidden on a corner on Dempster, but once you walk inside it opens into a fantastic combination of rich coffees, bottled drinks (including the Coca-Cola Classic) and a great place to sit and really feel welcome.

500 Main
(847) 328.7940
Main

Kafein

One of the only places in Evanston open after midnight, Kafein appeals to the late-night college crowd with a jukebox, plush couches and little tables used for studying. The restaurant's art emphasizes caffeine as a drug of choice, with pictures of lines of ground coffee and black liquid in a hypodermic needle. The menu features plenty of ways to get your fix including mugs of spiced Mexican hot chocolate, sweet white mocha shakes and huge cups of espresso.

1613 Central
(847) 864.2700
Davis

10 Evanston

to play. Evanston

(Body) = Chemis+ri

The success of this store is based in its individual style and contemporary stock. A book store, spa, body shop and clothing store wrapped into one, anyone can find anything to relax and feel good. If you are stressed with school, work, friends, and, well, life in general, stop by. Man or woman, this store will make you feel like a new person in less time and with less money than most spend at a spa.

613 Dempster
(847) 424.1790
Dempster

Dave's Down to Earth Rock Shop and Prehistoric Life Museum

This expansive wonderland of crystals, minerals, fossils and shells brings out the rock collector in anyone. Along the walls are racks of necklaces, shelves of intricate seashells and miniature fossils, and endless bins containing everything from copper spheres to polished semiprecious stones.

In the store's interior, glass displays house glittering jewelry and crystals at every price. A trip to the creepy museum in the basement is also a must, to witness trilobites and dinosaur bones amidst eerie background music.

1520 Sherman
(847) 733.8300
Davis

Bar Louie

From 5 p.m. to close Tuesday nights, Bar Louie caters to hungry college students and the Evanston after-work crowd who chow down on dollar burgers with soda, beer or custom martinis. The burgers come with lettuce, but other toppings and sides like fries and onion rings are extra and worth the cost. Despite the crowd, service is quick, with staff members practically patrolling the tables, bar and outdoor patio to keep the food and drinks coming.

1520 Sherman
(847) 733.8300
Main

Nevin's Pub

Nevin's Pub is more than just a place to pack in some carbs before a night of drinking. Whether you're with the college crowd seeing a local band performing at the bar or catching a beer on your lunch break, the plush leather chairs and quick service make the Irish style pub a great place to eat. The food is good quality, with classics like greasy plates of potato skins, fish and chips and heaping salad with fresh strawberries and salmon.

1450 N. Sherman
(847) 869.0450
Dempster

Evanston 11

to shop.

...ber, Rubber Ducky, On Vinyl, Green Day, Vintage Channel Purse, Fire Polished, Cowbo...

Possibilities

Every touristy town has a shop like this: pretty silver jewelry, specialty soaps, and a wall of weird novelty items like "growing" sponge dinosaurs.

Seemingly themeless, Possibilities offers unique, random gift ideas for the friend who has everything. From lovely beaded purses to creepy Elvis finger puppets, you're guaranteed to find something of interest in this bizarre retailer.

1235 Chicago
(847) 328.1235
Dempster

Another Time Another Place

A visit here is like a visit to grandma's attic. You can look, but don't touch. The store carries everything from antique furniture, to jewelry, to vintage clothing, to unusual postcards. For college students looking to decorate their apartments with one-of-a-kind posters, try the old magazine advertisements, like the Lucky Strike ad that says smoking will keep you looking young. For that matter, you could even furnish your entire apartment here! Make sure you check out every nook and cranny. You might just find that wooden train set you always wanted.

1243 Chicago
(847) 866.7170
Chicago

Beadazzled

This tiny bead store, about the size of a college dorm room, is perfect for the college student looking to give a gift with a personal touch. Whether you are looking for something fun and affordable for a friend or something more elegant for your mom, this store has it all.

And you don't have to be particularly artistic to put something together. The store sells books and magazine about beading. Also, the store offers classes on everything from basic bead stringing to advanced bead crocheting for a fee.

2002 Central
(847) 864.9494
Central

Council Thrift Shop

This is your run-of-the-mill, stereotypical thrift shop. Housed in a decrepit little corner store, this church-run shop offers mounds of yellowing paperbacks, boxes of mismatched silverware and overstuffed racks of mostly hideous clothing. There are hidden treasures if you're willing to dig deep and ignore the funny smell. It's worth a stop if you're already in the neighborhood, but doesn't merit its own trip

1524 W. Howard
(773) 764.2364
Howard

Beadazzled

Secret Treasures Antiques

As soon as you step foot into this quaint shop, you feel as if you discovered a hidden North Shore treasure. The owners are constantly going to moving sales, estate auctions and tiny, random stores to collect the items in this shop. From doilies to stunning turquoise jewelry, they have it all. This is a great place to buy gifts for a mother, grandmother, or guy friend with impeccable taste. Otherwise, just browse and take in the scenery.

611 Dempster
(847) 866.6889
Dempster

Evanston

Viva Vinatage

Standing out beyond the trends, Viva Vintage is known for its classic vintage clothes. Nothing is overpriced and the owner takes pride in choosing clothes that are in mint condition and wearable. There are the obligatory '80s picks and some retro T-shirts, but Viva Vintage also houses a mess of men's and women's pants, tops, jewelry, shoes and accessories. Buy some huge old sunglasses and a cigarette holder, and bask in the time warp.

 1043 Chicago
(847) 475.5025
Main

Cottage Jewelry

Cottage Jewelry has a family room feel with a friendly staff that keeps a Labrador behind the counter. Whether you're looking to get something repaired, pick up some simple sterling earrings or a high end gift for your mother's birthday, the prices are reasonable but bartering is encouraged. While the shop is small, there's a selection of antique and custom designed jewelry so you can make sure you get a unique piece.

 530 Dempster
(847) 328.1420
Dempster

2nd Hand Tunes

2nd Hand Tunes is a relief from Evanston's chain retail music selection. Skip Barnes and Noble and Borders and go straight to 2nd Hand Tunes for a respectable collection of used music and artist posters. It's a small store, but the guy who runs the place is almost always there, ready to help you in your search for that CD or LP you'll be listening to for the rest of the week.

 800 Dempster
(847) 491.1690
Dempster

The Mexican Shop

Into trends but sick and tired of looking like a cookie-cutter clone? The Mexican Shop has you covered. From psychedelic circa-1970s wire desk ornaments to the classic Audrey Hepburn floppy hat, this store will have you dressing to the nines without breaking into your savings. Hollywood jewelry, hats of every color and size, full and fun shirts and blouses, and an honest, truly helpful staff will make you a sworn regular after your first trip.

 801 Dempster
(847) 475.8665
Dempster

Accents Plus

Although you can find a cute tank top or trendy purse if you look carefully, the majority of clothes in this store look like the flashy ensembles your grandmother wears on a summer day. The clothing colors are bold, so don't be surprised when you find a polka-dotted blazer or a long shirt that looks like a kimono. Students should probably skip browsing around the store and just check out the reasonably priced, cute jewelry near the front counter.

 601 Davis
(847) 864.0420
Davis

Evanston 13

Rogers Park

to eat.......................Ayra Bhavan
                        Ennui Café
                        Café Descartes
to shop.....................Unan Imports
                        Patel Brothers
                        Under The Table Books
to play.....................Dilshad
                        The Side Project
                        Sweet Music Studio

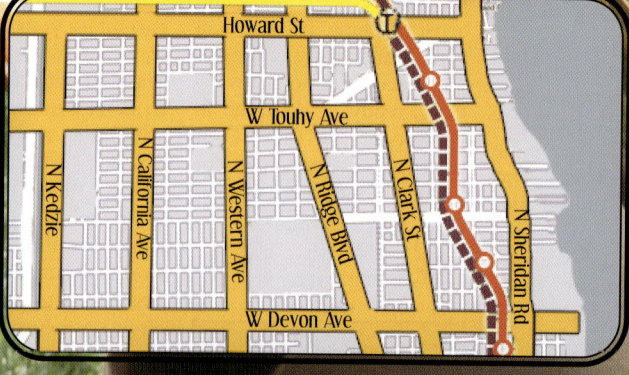

Unzipped

With 63,000 residents speaking 80 languages, Rogers Park doesn't have one face or one identity.

rogers park.

Its jazzy, beatnik, activist spirit pulsates through each inhabitant, through Loyola University and through the 13 beaches and ten parks.

You can see it on Devon Street, Chicago's "Little India." Devon illuminates the heterogenic, harmonious population in Rogers Park.

You can see it at Heartland Cafe, the core of community activism. It represents Rogers Park's jazz and style with live musicians and its own activist publication and radio station.

You can see it at the NeighborFood Fest in Warren Park, where the community celebrates Chicago's motto, City in a Garden. The festival embodies the environmentally-concerned Rogers Park, which protects its waterfront from urban development.

You can see it in Julie Marcus, who opened Under the Table Books off the Jarvis el stop, a location under scrutiny.

Located along the Howard, Jarvis, Morse and Loyola el stops, Rogers Park offers a haven from a hectic lifestyle. The beaches, parks, beatnik cafes, outdoor festivals and live jazz performances provide repose and entertainment.

The crime in Rogers Park is being combated, but the violence is still real. Visitors should stick to well-lit areas. When safety precautions are taken, the Rogers Park spirit will be found.

But watch out. It's contagious.

www.ChicagoUnzipped.com

to eat.

wheat Cakes, All American Date, Rasgulla, Dom's Mom Focaccia, Mambo Italiano, Hawai

Jalebi: Think of it as a super sweet, thin Indian funnel cake. It's a standard Indian sweet that you can find at Sukadia **2559 West Devon**, (773) 338.5400, **Loyola (el) to 155 to Western (bus)** the garlic and will keep your date happy. On weekends, the buffet is open giving you a taste of everything.

 2508 W. Devon
(773) 274.5800
155 Devon, 49B Western, 84 Peterson (bus)

Panini Panini

Panini Panini is a little Europe shoved into Rogers Park. While a fast-paced world whirls outside its fence, Panini Panini offers European lunchtime calmness. Twenty-something foreign men push tables together and play poker for hours, talking rapidly in their native language while other customers read books and sip cappuccinos. The meal portions are too large and thick, but the drinks and desserts are fantastic mid-day treats. European music hums in the background, setting a quiet atmosphere for relaxed studying or lackadaisical poker-watching.

 6764 N. Sheridan
(773) 761.7775
147 to Columbia

Arya Bhavan

Ayra Bhavan is one of the few Indian restaurants serving all vegetarian dishes from north and south India. Really hungry and need an Indian food fix? After five bites you will feel full. The food is spicy but tolerable only if you can keep from lunging at the water pitcher. Try the onion bread (paratha); it's just as good as

Fluky's

A Fluky's dog is the ultimate Chicago-style Vienna Beef hot dog. Old-fashioned street posts decorate the restaurant, reminiscent of past Chicago hot dog "hot spots." Arcade games and wall jukeboxes bring out the 12-year-old in each of us. Combining a Fluky's visit with a trip to Warren Park's batting cages makes the perfect all-American date or all-American night out with the guys. Service is slow, but

Rogers Park

the great eats and friendly charm make Fluky's worth the trip.

6821 N. Western
(773) 274.3652
49B to Pratt

Ennui Cafe

If you're missing homemade cooking, Ennui Cafe's Shut Up & Eat dinners present the solution. On the weekend Ennui opens its back room and serves hearty, predetermined menus including Salisbury steak and peach cobbler. The room intimately seats 16 people. Regularly serving as a soup-and-sandwich cafe, Ennui illustrates the community's beatnik style, with misfit furniture and free live band performances on Wednesday, Friday and Sunday. It presents the annual

Rogers Park Jazz Series in August, an outdoor community fest featuring local bands.

6981 N. Sheridan
(773) 973.2233
Morse

Café Suron

A sky-blue ceiling, open wood-paneled windows, antique candelabras, delicate tablecloths and a stone fountain make Café Suron breezy and welcoming. It's like eating at an outdoor café in the Mediterranean. Service is pleasant and attentive; the owner walks around offering dish suggestions. The Hawaiian Tilapia, Fessenjan and Dolmeh Hummus are all musts. Schedule dinner when the Flamenco dancers perform. They study in Spain and return with a new repertoire.

1146 W. Pratt
(773) 465.6500
Morse

Kaffeccino

Addicted to Starbucks but feeling bored sipping the same mocha in the familiar cliché cup? Try Kaffeccino. It offers the standard coffee flavors but also smoothie and juice choices. Living room couches are located by the storefront window to relax and study. You can eat and drink while sitting on these; just don't put your dirty shoes on them.

Kaffeccino makes boxed lunches, breakfast trays and party trays, perfect for the student on the go, morning office meetings, or Saturday night's fiesta.

6441 N. Sheridan
(773) 508.1888
Loyola

Heartland Cafe

The soul of Rogers Park pulses through the Heartland Cafe. The community's activism, jazz and earthy vibe are reflected here in the wholesome food, political wall posters, beatnik furniture and live music. This locally popular stop is part of the "heart of Rogers Park." The Cafe supports a progressive journal and radio station, general store, theater and bar. The enlightening atmosphere and liberally rich culture still hold from the Heart's

opening in the 70s, making it a must-see.

 7000 N. Glenwood
(773) 465.8005
Morse

Café Descartes

Café Descartes brews a mean bean at a cheap price. Two machines that look like they've been taken from Charlie and the Chocolate Factory process beans at the front of the store. Descartes serves as a bean grinding laboratory and is shut down mid-morning so its coffee blends can be delivered to shops throughout the city. Coffee bean bags are strewn across the floor, giving the café a factory feel. Located under the Morse el stop, it's perfect for the morning commuter.

 1355 W. Lunt
(773) 262.7860
Morse

Morseland

A classy, smooth, and jazzy night on the town starts and ends at Morseland. Soft lighting, wood counters and burgundy velvet curtains create the ambiance of an old-fashioned piano bar. Morseland has an extensive bar, dining room area, pool table room and a stage for live music. Two VIP booths directly in front of the stage are perfect for an intimate evening, if you make reservations in advance. The restaurant combines dining and music every night.

 1218 W. Morse
(773) 764.8900
Morse

Heartland Cafe

Loyola Park

rogers park.

Rogers Park 19

to shop.

erba Daisy, Bhangra, Henna, Accordion, Harry Potter, Hibiscus, Bollywood, Raath Rani

Al-Mansoor Video

Al-Mansoor staff members jump at the chance to voice opinions on the latest Indian music styles. They send you out the door with only the best albums. This Indian video and music shop sells popular Hindi film soundtracks and Indian Idol winner Abhijeet Sawant's new album. Racks of cheap regional CDs and tapes fill the store's aisles, offering tunes from Kannada to Punjab. Photos of the owner with famous Indian stars modestly decorate the glass cabinets.

2600 W. Devon
(773) 764.7576
155 to Rockwell

Patel Brothers

Fifty-six ceramic jugs filled with dried Indian goods occupy the center aisle of Patel Brothers. The equivalent of a large chain grocery store, Patel Brothers sells Indian seeds, powders and spices, frozen foods and ready-made dinners. At least 17 types of lentils line one of the four double-sided aisles of cubby holes stocked with food. The vegetables and goods here can't be found anywhere else. Ready-made samosas and Maggi Noddles offer a tasty alternative to the typical ramen noodle trap.

2610 W. Devon
(773) 262.7777
155 to Rockwell

Unan Imports

At Unan Imports, all goods come from Africa: the clothing, toys, jewelry, instruments, lotions and decorations - except for the scarves. "I cheat a little," says store owner AS Ntamere. A huge selection of African masks, machetes and earrings hang on the walls, and dozens of African drums, thumb pianos and chess sets rest on the floor. Prices are cheap - a hand-carved instrument sells for $15. Ntamere may make you dance if you inquire about the drums.

6971 N. Sheridan
(773) 274.4022
Morse

Newleaf Natural Grocery

Stepping into Newleaf is like stepping into a Tom Hanks/Meg Ryan film: comfortable, quaint and warm. With aging wooden walls and floors, this grocery store transports you from the city to the country. All products, from nuts and vegetables to ice cream, are organic. Stop in for a sandwich and eat at the table by the window. Make sure to try Maude's carrot cake. The fruit is a bit pricey but so is the price of organic food.

1261 W. Loyola
(773) 743.0400
Loyola

Patel Brothers

20 Rogers Park

Rogers Park

Loyola Park

Blossom Flowers & Gifts

Got a date tomorrow and have no creativity? Want to surprise your date with a bouquet? Step into the greenhouse-like Blossom Flowers & Gifts. They make floral arrangements for any event at all prices. The staff is extremely helpful and makes planning enjoyable and simple. Flowers come from around the country daily and all bouquets are fresh. Greeting cards, jewelry, candles and wind chimes sold here will add spice to your gifts. They also gift wrap and deliver.

 7013 N. Sheridan
(773) 761.5611
147 to Lunt

Flatts & Sharpe's Music Company

Circular, triangular, square-shaped, tie-dye, glow-in-the-dark and brand-name guitar picks consume the glass counter at this music supply store's entrance. Test out guitar straps and shake maracas and decorated tambourines. An antique Round Records neon sign hangs in the back room, filled with voice, guitar and piano sheet music including tunes from Norah Jones to the Eurhythmics. The staff offers guitar, piano, cello and bass lessons for all skill levels.

 6749 N. Sheridan
(773) 465.5233
147 to Columbia

Sukhadia's Sweets and Snacks

For authentic Indian sweets, Sukhadia's is it. With zesty aromas in the air and a Hindu flower decoration hanging above the register, this is as close to India as you can get

Reham's

without leaving Chicago. This family-run shop and catering service creates fresh snacks each day and offers novelties imported from India. The homemade Jalebi (a yellow, sugary candy shaped like a funnel cake) is a must-try. Imported Thumbs Up cola and pistachio Kulfi (Indian popsicle) are refreshing alternatives to American equivalents.

2559 W. Devon
(773) 338.5400
155 to Rockwell

Sona Chandi

Remember those Indian beaded slip-on clogs popular chain stores tried to replicate? Sona Chandi carries the real deal. For $20, you can leave Devon Avenue with a pair of real Indian sandals that will stick out from the imposters. Sona Chandi, however, sells mostly jewelry and various boutique outfits. The bindis are numerous and varied in style, from simple single beads to starburst shapes. If you need to spice up that little black dress, these add the perfect flair.

2637 W. Devon
no phone
155 to Washtenaw

Resham's

Multi-colored fabrics decorated with beads, starbursts and swirls hang from the ceiling at Resham's. This clothing and sari shop pops out from the rest because of its wide selection of fabric textures and styles. While the Kurtis (Indian shirts) are the biggest sellers, the shiny bangles and beaded belts could spice up any outfit. Resham's also sells duvet covers, adding artistic flavor to your cell-like dorm or apartment. Inventive shoppers can purchase fabrics by the yard and create new fashions.

2540 W. Devon
(773) 764.9692
155 to Rockwell

Rakhee: On a special Indian holiday, brothers tie this bracelet on their sisters to represent that they will always protect and take care of their sisters.

The Armadillo's Pillow

It is like stepping into one of JRR Tolkien's fantastical hobbit homes. Stacks of ancient used books extend to the golden swirled, round ceiling. The combination of old Victorian furniture, beaded Indian pillows and

The coffee machine: These machines are behind your morning jolt of caffein.

22 Rogers Park

plush purple drapes create the perfect ambiance for enjoying that hard-to-find book. Most noticeable is the store's sense of humor. Sections range from "Magic and Spells" to "Books of Possible Interest to the Homesteader." New books brought in daily.

6753 N. Sheridan
(773) 761.2558
147 to Columbia

Under The Table Books

This used book store has a great homey feel. The owner's favorite place to read was, "under my dining room table." Her father's ancient typewriter and desk lamp sit on display in the front window and a resident dog, Rocky, gives readers some company. What you read here could very well become reality. The "New Guide to Rome: 1968" contained a 1969 Italy parking pass, and "Chicago's Wildest Hobohemian Nightspots"

can send you venturing around the city.

1443 W. Jarvis
(773) 743.3728
Jarvis

Caribbean American Baking Company

Go a little out of your way to fill up on peppery meat and veggie pies (a.k.a. patties), oily sweet bread and heavy cakes. No cornball music, no fake rastas, just a family bakery. The Caribbean American Baking Company is a fixture for the locals, so have a little fun pretending you know what

you're doing: tuck the house favorite, the beef patty, inside the coco bread. There's no in-house seating, which is inconvenient, but its goodies are worth the trip for take-out.

1539 W. Howard
(773) 761.0700
Howard

Rogers Park 23

Lost Eras

Standing at the cash register, owner Charlotte Walters yells for her employee who is at the back of the store. Her speaking voice would merely be muffled by the 14,000 square foot showroom, stuffed to the max with costumes, wigs, masks and antiques.

"Irv? Irv. Come up here and price these teacups," Walters shouts as she hands a customer one of the 400 antique fans the store just acquired from a dealer.

Lost Eras buys and sells antiques from around the world, and rents and sells costumes to Chicago theaters and individual shoppers. A 19 room rehearsal studio upstairs provides practice space for Chicago musicians. The front of Lost Eras displays antique furniture, rugs, ovens, 1940s radios and 1950s Playboys that the store buys and sells.

"It's not like one of those consignment shops where you pick [costumes] out of a catalogue," Walters said, straightening the Victorian rings on the front counter. "Psh. That's so passé. You'll find things here that you'd only find in museums."

While Lost Eras deals items from the past, it holds a rich history all its own. The basement served as a speakeasy in the 1920s and featured musicians such as Ella Fitzgerald.

"The booze was coming in through the back," Walters said, pointing behind the cash register to a staircase leading to the basement. The numbered hooks in the speakeasy's coat room can still be seen.

Walters' mother opened a "head shop" in the space in 1969, selling, "psychedelic stuff," Walters said. Walters claims that several ghosts reside in Lost Eras today.

"Some people say it's haunted. One psychic was here and said three ghosts were in the basement and one was in the attic," Walters said. "I [wouldn't doubt it] considering the illegal activity that was going on here." Irving Watts, Lost Eras employee of 15 years, emerges from behind two racks of French maid costumes.

"It's weird. There's a clock that's never wound but rings everyday," Watts said, pointing to a small wooden clock at the front of the store. " 'Dong, dong.' It only does it at 4 o'clock."

to play.

Macerena, Threading, Hotdog, Mission Impossible, Extra Buttery Popcorn, Refuge from

Warren Park

Outdoor batting cages with pitching machines, one ice rink, five baseball diamonds, one sledding hill, six tennis courts, one 9-hole golf course, skate ramps, basketball courts, open fields, and 98 acres make Warren Park a must-visit in Rogers Park. One coin from the field house will get you 15 pitches in the batting cages. Need a break from all activity? The rolling hills and expansive open space provide quiet refuge in the city.

6601 N. Western
(773) 262.6314
49B to Western

Dilshad

A Dilshad "threader" uses a spool of thread in ways a fairy godmother would exercise her wand. Wishing to eliminate unwanted facial hairs, customers without appointments walk into the store, sit in a chair and are threaded within minutes. The threader uncurls a piece of string and weaves it meticulously across unwanted hairs, removing fuzz crisply and painlessly. Service is quick and cheap, and just watching the threader is mesmerizing.

2645 W. Devon
(773) 761.5740
155 to Rockwell

The Side Project

Located just off the Jarvis el stop, the small and dimly lit Side Project is easily unnoticed by passers-by. But this 32-seat venue is continuously producing ambitious new plays written and directed by Chicagoans. This theater accepts submissions for one-act scripts and staged readings, which are performed throughout the year. The original works and personal atmosphere create the perfect intimate setting for an avant-garde date.

1520 W. Jarvis
(773) 973.2150
Jarvis

Loyola Park

Loyola Park proves the perfect getaway from daily monotony. Service stations dot the jogging path, each detailing a different cardiovascular exercise. Lake Michigan beach, an arching, glacial-like sculpture and the break wall (a canvas in the annual Artists of the Wall Festival, where every summer novice and expert artists pay a $30 entry fee and paint a chunk of the wall assigned to them) are great for relaxing. The true jazzy, cultural and nature-oriented

26 rogers park

Rogers Park

, Belly Dancing, , Eyeshadow, Lin

Rogers Park shines through in this masterpiece.

1230 W. Greenleaf
(773) 262.8605
147 to Greenleaf

Sweet Magic Studio

The Hand Jive and the Macarena may have impressed friends in 6th grade, but its time to expand your dance repertoire. Why not try belly dancing? Sweet Magic Studio offers beginner belly dance courses in a six-week session. You may want to limber up with some yoga classes, which are the studio's specialty. Yoga is taught by Kareena, an instructor with 40 years of experience. Get your hips moving, and you're sure to own the dance floor at the next party.

6960 N. Sheridan
(773) 764.6488
Morse

Village North Theater

You can't miss the flashy, traffic-light green Village North Theater sign on Sheridan Road. This theater prides itself on being one of the three Chicago theaters with the cheapest first-run show tickets. It offers a cozy family feel. Movies can even be heard from the foyer. Old movie posters and giant Roy Lichtenstein artworks line the hallways. There are four theaters to house a total 609 people. Village North is nothing fancy, but it's a great deal for your money.

6746 N. Sheridan
(773) 764-.9100
147 to Columbia

Uptown

What ever happened

to eat.....................The No Exit Café
　　　　　　　　　　The Urban Tea Lounge
　　　　　　　　　　Crew Bar & Grill

to shop....................Tattoo Factory
　　　　　　　　　　"Z" Wallis Discount
　　　　　　　　　　Shake, Rattle & Read

to play....................Aragon Ballroom
　　　　　　　　　　Uptown Lounge
　　　　　　　　　　Riviera Theatre

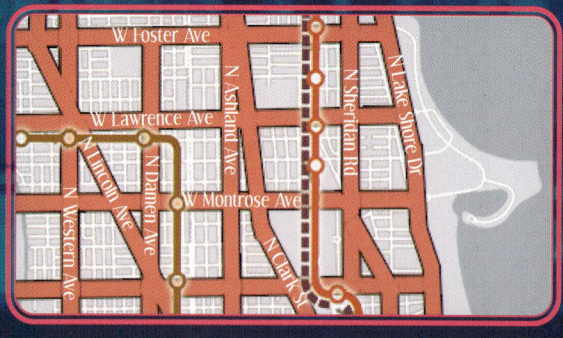

Chicago Unzipped

Unzipped to Hollywood?

Like a talented actor who'll play any role, Uptown is a neighborhood of many identities. Before Hollywood became the world's movie Mecca, Uptown produced many of the country's feature films at Essanay and other studios. Movie stars and mobsters alike roamed the streets throughout the early 1900s, often meeting at the theaters and speakeasies centered at Lawrence and Broadway. During this golden age, it's said that the crowds filing out from the Uptown, Riviera and Aragon on late Saturday nights made the intersection look like Times Square on New Year's Eve.

Today, Uptown has an edgy-but-evolving feel that's more akin to western Brooklyn. There are up-and-coming areas, beautiful historic spots, and some blocks to avoid entirely. The mass exodus to suburbia after World War II that impoverished the neighborhood reversed in the 1900s, and now an alphabet soup of community improvement groups fight to put Uptown on equal footing with affluent neighbors like Lakeview and Edgewater.

Economic disparities linger and Uptown remains home to a disproportionate number of social services and low-income houses. But the undercurrents that made Uptown an artistic hub still flow. The neighborhood's brilliant architecture, diverse population, and lower rents attract many artists, writers, and other creative types. Uptown also boasts the People's Music School, where free music lessons are available for anyone who desires. Lawrence and Broadway is even reemerging as the neighborhood hot spot, however, only time will tell whether Uptown can regain its movie star shine.

The Red line

Lawrence

Lawrence lies in the heart of Uptown's entertainment district. Legends like the Aragon, Green Mill and Riviera are within easy walking distance, as are neighborhood newcomers Borders and Starbucks. The high platform is a great place to admire Uptown's breathtaking architecture.

Wilson

Wilson Yard was a CTA repair station before a massive 1996 fire burnt it to the ground. Vacant for nearly a decade, the city recently green-lighted a proposal to develop the lot into subsidized housing featuring a Target and a 14-screen movie theater. Until then do not hang out here at night.

runs through it.

The Red Line's three Uptown stops get you almost anywhere you want to go and provide insight into the neighborhood's changing character.

Argyle

The Vietnamese, Cambodian and Laotian signs may make you double-take as you exit onto Argyle's pagoda-sporting platform. The street greets you with an excellent selection of authentic Asian restaurants and shops. Get your fill but be careful on the ride home - there's been a rash of drug arrests at the station recently.

to eat.

The Twins, Oolong tea, Lounge, Don't Dent the Wallet, Minor Arcana, Papua New Guinea

Sun Wah Bar-B-Q Restaurant

Don't let the dead ducks swinging in the window scare you. Sun Wah roasts up some of the best birds in town. Those fowl on display are like a freshness guarantee. Poultry, seafood, pork, beef and rice plates are served in sizes meant for sharing, so bring friends. The wait staff is friendly if not exactly fluent, but sometimes absent. Be prepared to gesticulate, and wait. It'll be worth it - the roasted duck is as good as advertised.

1132 Argyle
(773) 769.1254

Argyle

Thai Pastry

Thai Pastry is a favorite in Uptown and throughout Chicago, evidenced by the numerous four-star reviews that line the restaurant's front window. Owner Aumphai Kusub serves up big portions of curries, stir fried noodles and rice at student-friendly prices. The spice-adverse should be careful - even their "mild" curry has a kick. Cool down with bubble tea, a deliciously bizarre, big-strawed slushy with sneaky tapioca balls. Spending more than $10 gets you a free pastry and the chance to waddle home stuffed but happy.

4925 N. Broadway
(773) 784.5399

Argyle

Crew Bar and Grill: Combining sports, homosexuality and quality food is a tall order, but Crew is all about blending the exotic. Their flamboyant menu offers creative twists on pub-grub favorites, including a BLT that features jalapeno cream cheese and red onions. Crew also has more than 40 microbrews from around the globe. Servers are predictably attentive to good looking males, but can be snooty towards others. The only sports bar you'll find that will shun the playoffs for Desperate Housewives.
4804 N. Broadway, 773-784-2739, **Argyle**

The No Exit Cafe

No Exit Café is a place where Dean Moriarty could have hung out, but probably didn't. It was opened 50 years ago by two Northwestern students. Though No Exit has died many times since, it's back again. Today, the new, clean café serves coffee with film screenings, soulful jazz music and open-mic Mondays. Ever feel like you are in a rut as far as the "college experience?" Chill here to relocate that vibe.

6970 N. Glenwood
(773) 743.3355

Morse

Hon Kee

Take a small town diner, turn it into a Chinese restaurant and you've got something like Hon Kee. It's easy to miss this place while wandering Argyle Street, but don't pass it by. Drop in for the quickie barbeque or take a seat: the décor is unsavory,

32 Uptown

Uptown

...but as soon as you sit down expect a smile from the server, a cup of tea and a menu full of simple, heavily flavored Chinese dishes.

1064 W. Argyle
(773) 878.6650
Argyle

The Urban Tea Lounge

This is why you moved to city: to find hip, off-the-beaten-path places with a welcoming atmosphere and an exotic touch. The Urban Tea Lounge baits you with smooth, aromatic teas from around the globe then holds you with its comfy lounge, brilliant décor, friendly staff and inexpensive lunch options (pint and sandwich, $5). Try their Monkey Harvest Yunnan, a black tea harvested by trained Chinese monkeys. Visit on Friday between 4 and 9 p.m. to hear your future from their Tarot reader!

838 W. Montrose
(773) 907.8726
145 to Broadway

Metropolis Coffee Company: Whether you want to nurse a tall latte over your laptop or pick up a fresh batch of micro-roasted beans, this Edgewater coffee house is there to lovingly prepare your daily caffeine fix. The menu of coffee (roasted on the premises) rotates often, and you'll always be able to find organic and free-trade options. Munchable sandwiches work well with the gourmet espresso drinks. The staff knows their coffee and is willing to chat about anything from bean varieties to the café's eclectic music.
1039 W. Granville, (773) 764.0400, **Granville**

Uptown 33

to shop.

ssession, White, Sugar, Lithography, Vintage Pornography, Charcoal & Graphite, Japan

Tattoo Factory

Chicago's oldest tattoo parlor got a makeover this summer. Since 1976, Tattoo Factory has pierced, pricked and painted permanent body art onto thousands of satisfied (though perhaps sore) customers at its loud, garish, brilliant neon shop on Broadway. The Wilson Yard housing project forced Tattoo Factory to move across the street, but the new parlor will be three times as large, have big screen TVs, and remain home to some of the city's best artists.

4441 Broadway
(773) 989.4077
Wilson

"Z" Wallis Discount Department

Not sure what to wear to next week's army-themed frat party? This is the place to go, especially for a cheap find. This hole-in-the-wall discount surplus store is stuffed with new and used army/navy apparel along with authentic vintage buttons and patches. This place is great even for the true military person, selling all types of paraphernalia, from outdoor supplies to camouflage shoelaces.

4647 N. Broadway
(773) 784.9140
Wilson

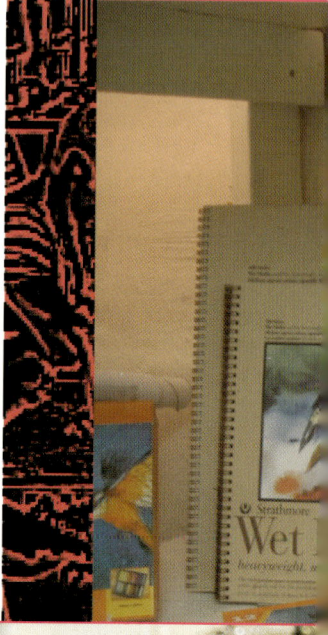

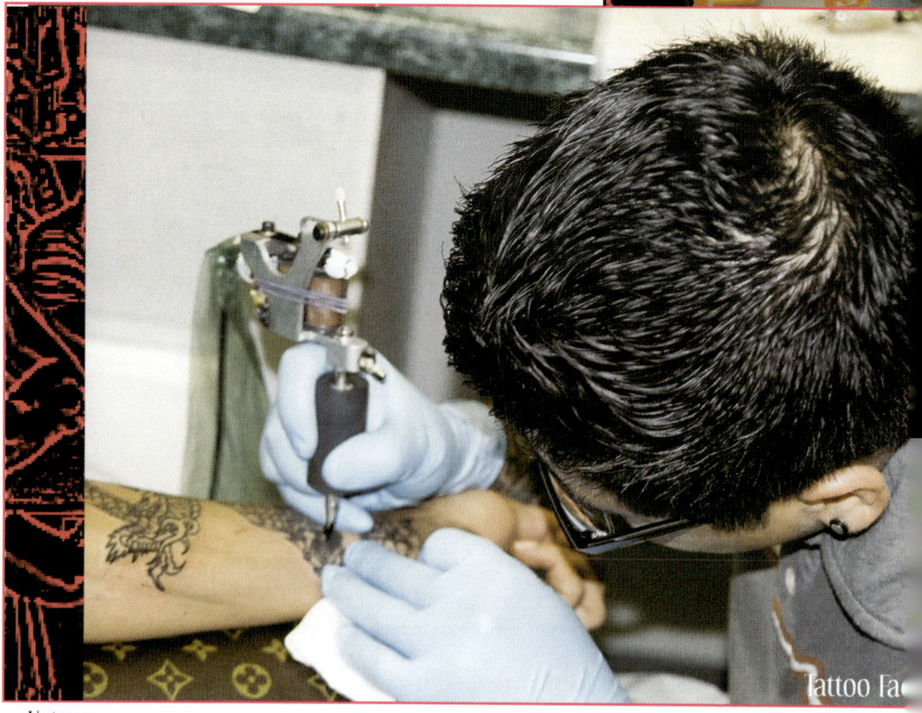

Tattoo Fa

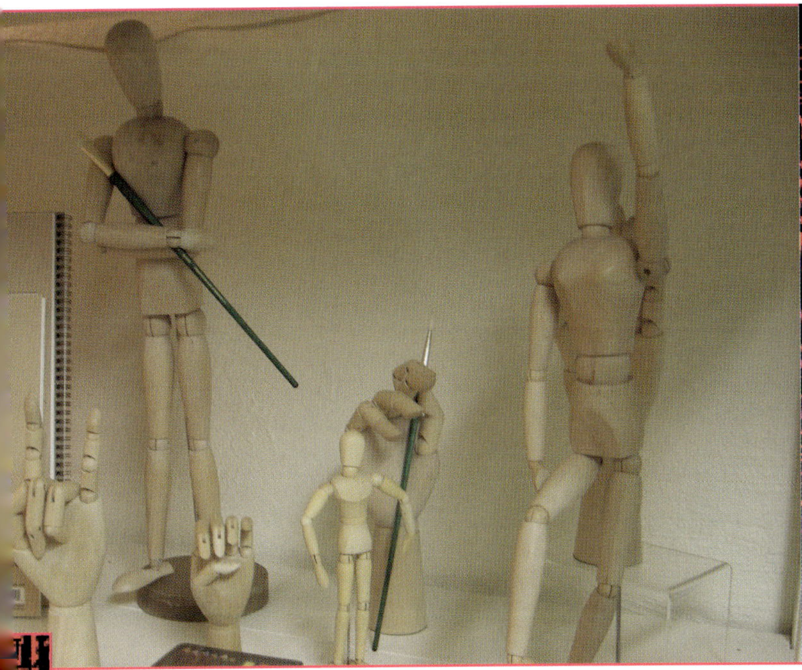

Uptown

Suit Tattoo, Gouache,   Origami, Alyssa Milano, Cerleua

Artcetera: If you're looking for affordable art supplies, want to create beautiful pieces of art to decorate your apartment, or just need another activity to fill time while avoiding homework, then Artcetera, the Edgewater art store, is the place for you. Owner Tori Wise sells art supplies and offers art classes for all levels. Though this requires you to spend a little dough, it will be all worth it to show off your artwork to the next date you bring home. **5301 N. Clark**, (773) 728.5301, **22 to Clark (bus)**

Shake, Rattle & Read

Shake, Rattle & Read is a treasure hunter's dream that will captivate you for as long as you can stand the stink of stale nicotine. Legendary musicians, including ex-Smashing Pumpkins singer Billy Corgan, have been known to browse the shop's stacks of yellowed paperbacks, racks of rare vinyl and shelves of vintage pornography. Bonus score if owner Ric Addy shows you the catacombs, a basement tunnel that links the store with the Green Mill and dates back to Al Capone's bootlegging days. Happy Hunting!

4812 N. Broadway
(773) 334.5311
Lawrence

Swedish Bakery

Filled with a delicious selection of rich European-style cakes and pastries at a price that's perfectly affordable for money-deprived college students. While it is a ten minute trek from the el and is usually crowded with patrons with no sit down room inside, the quality of their medley of goods overshadows the negatives. Their mini fruit topped cheesecake and cannolis are particularly yummy.

5348 N. Clark
(773) 561.8919
36 to Baltimore

Uptown 35

to play.

eteriorating, Live, Hillbilly, Spanish Palace Courtyard, Al Capone, Karaokee, Spotlight,

Aragon Ballroom

Aragon Ballroom is a castle or a cave, depending on who you ask. Architecturally, Aragon resembles old-world Spain, with terra-cotta ceilings and high arches. Acoustically, this cavernous converted warehouse can make headlining bands sound as if they're spelunking. Whether Aragon is hosting a sweat-soaked rock show or a rhythmic Latin dance night, its elevated stage offers tall fans an intimacy unavailable at arena shows. Shorter folks should head to the balcony for a better view.

 1106 W. Lawrence
(773) 561.9500
Lawrence

Frankie J's

How much entertainment can you pack into one address? This restaurant/theater/art gallery is as eclectic as its owner, Frankie J, a restaurateur, chef, comedian and magician who's a regular on the Food Network. The downstairs restaurant serves American fare comfort food, with pastas, hand-cut steaks and five different delicious salmon dishes. After dinner, the upstairs theater offers plays and both improvisational and sketch comedy. On Sundays the Methadome showcases and sells local artwork beginning at 4 p.m.

 4437 N. Broadway
(773) 769.2959
Wilson

The Green Mill

Sit in Al Capone's plush lounge seat at The Green Mill and you'll quickly see why the jazz club was the legendary gangster's favorite speakeasy. The dimly lit wooden walls and large oil landscape paintings provide a perfect atmosphere for enjoying some of the finest jazz in America. Keep 'yer yap shut during the show - loudmouths won't be served by the bar staff. On Sundays the club hosts a nationally-renowned poetry slam that's open to newcomers.

 4802 N. Broadway
(773) 878.5552
Lawrence

Uptown Lounge

Uptown Lounge represents the duality urban redevelopment, where improvement sometimes means loss of character. The building was once the ol' Saxony, possibly the divest of all dive bars, home to punkers, townies and other colorful late-nighters. New ownership gutted the place, sacrificing its carnival flavor for modern, antiseptic comforts. The new lounge is meticulously clean, and is a good spot to meet friends before and after shows at the Aragon or Riviera, but it has all the atmosphere of a dentist's waiting room.

 1136 W. Lawrence
(773) 878.1136
Lawrence

Big Chicks

You'll see naked women every night at Big Chicks, the friendliest gay bar in Chicago. The walls are covered with pictures of women in various states of undress, including a painting of the bar's owner, Michelle Fire. Big Chicks is a relaxed alternative to Boys' Town bars and welcomes people of all stripes, though most customers are males-seeking-

Uptown

males. Crowded weekend nights offer live DJs, dancing and free shots at midnight. The bartenders make mean Absolut martinis.

5024 N. Sheridan
(773) 728.5511
Argyle

Carol's Pub

Yee-haw! Saddle up and saunter down to Carol's for an adventure in southern hospitality. Seated in part of Uptown affectionately called "Hillbilly Heaven," Carol's offers plenty of cold beer, stiff whiskey, live country music, and possibly the best people-watching in Chicago. You won't blend in with the flannel-wearing, big-haired regulars, but you'll find them surprisingly welcoming. Expect to pay a visitor's premium for your pitchers of Old Style. Carol's band, Diamondback, features Nashville musicians who can flat-out jam. Thursday Karaoke is a must-see.

4659 N. Clark
(773) 334.2402
81 to Clark

Riviera Theatre: Moshing is so yesterday, but so is the Riviera. Once considered the finest cinema in Uptown, the Riv opened in 1918 for wealthier Chicagoans looking to enjoy shows in a family-friendly environment that featured a children's playroom and a nursing station. Today mosh pits keep nurses active at the theater, which is now one of Chicago's best rock concert halls. The Riv's former elegance is buried beneath layers of dirt and nicotine stains but the sound quality can't be beat. **4746 N. Racine**, (773) 275.6800, **Lawrence**

Lakeview

to eat:
La Batigue, Blue Bayou, Melrose Restaurant

to shop:
The Alley, Silver Moon, Wooden Spoon

to play:
Cherry Red, Spin, Cubby Bear

Unzipped

Wrigleyville scene...

to play: Wrigley Field

So, you want to watch a baseball game, maybe get a beer, but your significant other absolutely needs to get her shopping fix in today or else you'll be sleeping on the floor. Then Lakeview is the place for you! Often called Wrigleyville, thanks to the wonderful home of the Chicago Cubs, Wrigley Field, Lakeview is the place with just about everything. This neighborhood has the best nightlife concentration in the area outside of Rush Street downtown. But besides being a rowdy place, Lakeview also has an incredible array of shops and restaurants. A landmark of the restaurants includes the abundance of outdoor seating during the summer months.

Even more, Lakeview is the host to The Gay and Lesbian Pride Parade each year and caters to pretty much every crowd you can imagine. With young professionals crawling all over the place, Lakeview is the place to live for those who love the urban life. Transportation to and from the neighborhood makes this a very accessible place and thus a great place to live if you work in the Loop. Not to mention a Cubs game is just a short walk away. By being so flexible and diverse, Lakeview has managed to become the place to be and drop a couple bucks here and there.

lakeview.

to eat. Orange

www.ChicagoUnzipped.com

to eat.

Vienna, French Toast, Colored Meringues, Steak, Vanilla Lattes, Cajun Cuisine, Brown S

Pick Me Up Café

Finally, there's a place where both meat loving friends and vegans can enjoy a late night snack. Pick Me Up Café offers dishes well worth the price, from cakes to calamari to vegan French toast. Portions are big, and the quality of food sure beats any other local diner dishes prepared by tattooed servers. Walls and tables are adorned with various drawings and knick-knacks, giving the café an appearance of a time warped '50s diner.

3408 N Clark
(773) 248.6613
Belmont

Chicago Diner

A vegetarian and vegan haven located in Boystown. They offer everything a meat-eater could want like philly cheese steaks, patty melts, sloppy joes, and even faux-fish sandwiches. It is a tad on the pricey side, as most veg-friendly restaurants are, but it is definitely worth it. Several types of cakes and other baked goods are made in-house, along with plenty of milkshakes and smoothies to choose from.

3411 N Halsted
(773) 935.6696
Belmont

Ann Sather

It's nice to know that even in the heart of grungy Belmont, Ann Sather's is looking out for you. The hot meals are reasonably priced and the desserts are always included with the dinners. Breakfast is served all day, as are Sather's famous cinnamon rolls. The interior is cozy and the glow of lamplight off the dark wood warms you up without a cup of joe. Be sure to check out the portrait of Ann Sather herself that hangs over the hearth.

929 Belmont
(773) 348.2378
Belmont

Salt and Pepper Diner

Just a base run away from Wrigley Field, the Salt and Pepper Diner makes for a perfect eating spot before a game. With its traditional diner fare, from juicy hamburgers to chicken fingers, Salt and Pepper makes its customers long for the days of poodle skirts and jukeboxes. Salt and Pepper's offers its patrons a wide range of beverages as well. Try one of their chocolate milkshakes or grab a beer before the game.

3537 N Clark
(773) 883.9800
Addison

Cullen's Bar and Grille

With a little taste of Ireland mixed with a little taste of everything else, Cullen's Bar and Grille provides the perfect atmosphere for an after-work drink or cozy dinner with friends. From hefty hamburgers to succulent steaks, Cullen's is the perfect place to find a good meal of meat. Located on Southport Avenue, near several theaters and trendy bars, Cullen's also makes a good

40 Lakeview

Lakeview

eating spot before a night on the town.

3741 N Southport
(773) 975.0600
Southport

Julius Meinl

A little bit of Vienna is hiding in the midst of Chicago at Julius Meinl. The warmly painted walls and snug seating implores customers to remember that coffee should always be an indulgent experience. From groups of hipsters discussing worldly problems over soy vanilla lattes, to couples talking quietly across their exotic herbal teas, Julius Meinl's clientele is as varied as their selection of drinks. Be sure to try their freshly baked pastries and cakes-they will make your mouth water.

3601 Southport
(773) 868.1857
Southport

El Burrito Mexicano

Right off the Addison el stop, this shop lives up to its speedy namesake, providing fast and filling Mexican food for commuters on the go. As ethnic fare on-the-go has become more popular, El Burrito Mexicano gives its mainstream counterparts a run for their money. If you're not in a run, you can sit in and eat in the small seating section. With good prices and large portions, El Burrito Mexicano makes a perfect spot for economical eating.

936 W Addison
(773) 327.6991
Addison

Blue Bayou

Though the restaurant's vibrant art comes from the hands of New Orleans' artists and staples from the Big Easy are served like the famous Hurricane, Blue Bayou's menu is not limited to spicy Cajun cuisine. Four specialty dishes compile the Cajun fare, including jambalaya made with crawfish, chicken and Andouville sausage. The atmosphere sends you straight to Mardi Gras: beads hang from light fixtures, and karaoke and cover bands blast from the bar at night.

3734 Southport
(773) 871.3300
Southport

Taste of Heaven

Some may say it's pretty risky to name your cozy café Taste of Heaven. In this case, the name does not lie. Though pastel décor and scenic black and white stills on the wall may be modest, its menu is anything but. Dishes include curry chicken salad, softball size molasses spice cookies and the super sandwich Betty Crockeropolous. To die for: Jeanine's cake-torte with raspberries, blueberries and strawberries, whipped cream and cake crumbs in cream cheese frosting.

5401 N Clark
(773) 989.0151
22 to Balmoral

Hama Matsu

Hama Matsu does more than raw delivery by their female sushi chief. This dimly lit Asian restaurant serves traditional Japanese and Korean meals, so don't expect to dine on Asian-American dishes like Chicken Teriyaki. Since Hama Matsu's menu is heavy on flavors and does not shy away from being spicy, its knowledgeable staff will cater to individual palates. Got a tight budget? Parties of four or more can call ahead of time to discuss a dinner to fit their finances.

5143 N Clark
(773) 506.2978
22 to Foster (Bus)

Murphy's

Try a real Chicago hat dawg at Murphy's. Dat's right. Though da joint is tiny (red vinyl bar tables seat about 20), da dawgs are big. Dee's $3 puppies are meant to be eaten in twos. Murphy's also sells other Windy City favorites like brats, Italian sausage, homemade soup and triple thick shakes. And of course, Murphy's sports a TV for dose fans of da Cubs, da Bulls and da Bears.

1211 W Belmont
(773) 935.2882
Belmont

Matsu Yama

A sushi bar and restaurant, Matsu Yama is a simple and reasonably priced Japanese dining experience. What attracts people to Matsu Yama is the extensive sushi bar but the menu also features some traditional Japanese entrees. It is open late (usually until 1 a.m. during the week), BYOB and has valet parking.

1059 Belmont
(773) 327.8838
Belmont

Pops for Champagne

If you want to have an evening full of class, live jazz and champagne of pretty much any kind, Pops for Champagne is the place to go. This very upscale champagne and piano bar contains a stage with a bar around it for its nightly live music, a patio area open in the summer and a menu of fancy appetizers, cheeses, and desserts, and brunch on Sundays. Do not come here expecting a full menu of entrees or a cheap night out.

2934 N Sheffield
(773) 472.1000
Wellington

Pane Bread Café

Carb cutters beware; this quaint café specializes in sandwiches, pizza and pastas. The menu also includes a variety of salads and hummus. Some of the unique items you can find here are the bruschetta hummus and the garbage pizza. If you want to get your carb fix, come to Pane to have your bread of choice.

3002 N Sheffield
(773) 665.0972
Wellington

El Jardin

Big margaritas, inexpensive, traditional Mexican food and a friendly, laid back environment are the essentials that make up El Jardin. Filled with lively Latin music and colorful Mexican artwork, El Jardin caters to the entire Lakeview neighborhood. The usual crowd can range from families to young couples to baby boomers. During the summer, the restaurant's patio area is very popular among its patrons.

3335 N Clark
(773) 528.6775
Belmont

Orange

This trendy breakfast and lunch spot features brunch classics and unique dishes that are twists on some basics. Among these creative concoctions are the chai French toast, jelly donut pancakes and a triple-decker grilled cheese. With a moderately priced selection of foods, a kids menu, and a very homey environment, Orange is a place for everyone from young families to grandparents.

3231 N Clark
(773) 549.4400
Belmont

Duck Walk

This small but cozy Thai restaurant features great food that is enjoyable and inexpensive. With vegetarian and vegan options, this menu features your standard Thai cuisine that range in price from $6 to $8 for an entrée. Families and neighborhood regulars frequent Duck Walk, which displays unique artwork all over its walls. It is BYOB, there is no smoking at all in the restaurant and the menu is also available for delivery.

919 W Belmont
(773) 665.0455
Belmont

Melrose Restaurant

Melrose is a very popular dining spot among Chicago's gay scene and features basic but wonderful dinner food. The menu includes an international section that features various pastas, burgers, croissants, pie, seafood and breakfast is served all day. If you want to find a laid back and very friendly dining experience, you will most definitely find it at this simple American diner.

3233 N Broadway
(773) 327.2060
36 to Melrose (Bus)

La Creperie

If you can't already tell by the name, La Creperie specializes in crepes. The menu features all kinds of crepes, including the beef stroganoff crepe and the Nutella banana strawberry crepe. They also have a full wine and beer list and you can hear live music every Thursday night. This French style eatery, which has a patio that's open during the summer, is a great place to go to for a hearty meal and a romantic atmosphere.

2845 N Clark
(773) 528.9050
Wellington

Australian Homemade

This sterile ice cream and candy shop, which also has locations in New York and Australia, doesn't look very kid-friendly, nor are the prices child's play. But stop in for the most fun thing on the menu, the kid surprise cup: only $2 for one scoop of ice cream with a toy hidden in the underside of the cup. It's all tasty and worth the money if you can afford it, especially flavors like Green Apple sorbet, which tastes like frozen applesauce.

3425 Southport
(773) 281.3830
Belmont

Anthony's Homemade Italian Ice

Mike makes all the Italian Ice himself at Anthony's Homemade, and after tasting his creations, you'll want his autograph. The staff, eager to give out samples, will ask you to try the various flavors, like classic chocolate and a strawberry lemonade so authentic you can see the seeds. The ices taste exactly like their promised flavors, and you can enjoy the generous portions, which feel like well-packed snow in your mouth, inside the small, yellow-walled shop.

2009 Bissell
(773) 528.4237
Armitage

Uncommon Ground

Wait a minute...organic restaurants aren't supposed to be this good. Uncommon Ground is artsy and homey at once, with a menu that features not only vegetarian options but a Kobe beef burger as well. These juxtapositions make Uncommon Ground a des-

Lakeview 43

La Baguette: This bakery serves fresh traditional Mexican pastries and cakes to neighborhood regulars. Its glitzy outside beckons you to enter the wide-open bakery, whose windows are stacked with shelves of baked goods. Pick up a silver serving tray and a pair of tongs and serve yourself pastries such as brightly colored meringues and coconut-topped cookies all under $1 each. Ask your friendly baker about cakes for all occasions too. 5712 N Clark, **84 to Glenwood (bus)**

...tination for great food and excellent coffee. Enjoy the comfortable couch and the talkative staff, or come later and sit down at the expansive bar, which nearly cuts the space in half.

1214 W. Grace
(773) 929.3680
Sheridan

Samah

Samah, a hookah lounge, features 22 flavors of tobacco, including jasmine, mango and coffee. For $15, you'll get a beautifully decorated hookah, made with green glass and a gold tasseled hose. At Samah, you can smoke in near-privacy, as the long space is sectioned off with thick curtains that make the low mosaic table sur-rounded with throw pillows a hookah lover's mini-paradise. Don't overlook the food, either. The falafel is some of the best outside of the Middle East.

3330 N Clark
(773) 248.4606
Belmont

Bobtail Soda Fountain

This old-fashioned ice cream parlor was started by two University of Chicago students before they even graduated business school. With a back to basics approach on the ice cream shop, you will be able to find traditional flavors, sundaes and floats. They also have specialty flavors, including the Merlot Signature Sunset, which is non-alcoholic, and ice cream cakes and sandwiches. They also have a small but appealing café menu that contains a grilled peanut butter and jelly sandwich.

2951 Broadway
(773) 880.7372
Wellington

Root, Root, Root for the Cubbies!

"Root, root, root for the Cubbies, if they don't win it's a shame…" is a phrase that North Siders are born saying. Bleeding that Cubbie blue when baseball season starts, Cubs fans swarm to the physical manifestation of their emotional well-being and heartache, the beautiful ball park Wrigley Field.

Constructed in 1914, the second oldest ball park in America behind Fenway Park in Boston, Wrigley Field evokes nostalgia from long-time supporters and gets brand new fans thinking about why baseball is America's favorite past time. Vines of ivy sprawl across the outfield wall, giving the park its distinctive, classy look and the scoreboard-which has never been hit with a batted ball-is still manually operated. Traditions and superstitions run rampant around Wrigleyville: "Take me out to the ball game," a tune made famous in Chicago by beloved former announcer Harry Carey, is always sung before the 7th inning. Now celebrities and local heroes try their luck at leading the crowd to stay on key.

Before you step foot in the Friendly Confines, learn some Cubs etiquette: it is appropriate for fans to watch the game from the rooftops of surrounding buildings. Do not bring your pet billy goat with you for a day at Wrigley. Never, ever mention the name Bartman within 10 miles of the park. And speaking of unmentionables, to Cubs fans, there is only one true baseball team in Chicago.

Historic moments such as Babe Ruth's famous pointed home run in 1932, Ernie Bank's 500th career homer in 1970 and Kerry Wood's 20-strike out game in 1998 have all taken place at Wrigley. And even though the Cubs haven't won a World Series since 1908 and Sammy Sosa no longer swings for the home team, don't ever tell us that it's not our year.

Lakeview 45

… to shop.

… hnet Stockings, Paul Frank, Gemmed Rings, Rodeo Shirts, Bangles, Feather Boas, Clutch…

Medusa's Circle

Excess, electroclash and overindulgence are the three words that describe the grungy '80s acid trip atmosphere of Medusa's Circle. You expect Madonna to strut out from the pink leopard print dressing rooms wearing fishnets and mesh tanks. Some of the clothes can only be bought on a rock star budget but you must at least stop in to talk with owner Pierre. He'll chat about gold chains, invite you to a dance party or sell you a pin with his face on it.

3268 N Clark
(773) 935.5950
Belmont

Belmont Army/Navy Surplus

The three floor Army Surplus mega-store carries more than just fatigues. Music changes from floor to floor as you climb the staircase decorated with vintage war propaganda, army nets and brand stickers of casual designers like Paul Frank, Volcom and Diesel. Half of the third floor is flooded with fairly priced and sometimes completely worn vintage clothing. The other half is dedicated to camo. The shoe selection is perfect for any hipster, but shop around before laying the dollar down.

945 W Belmont
(773) 975.0626
Belmont

Uncle Fun

Uncle Fun is the ultimate goody bag store. A mishmash of knickknacks you thought were rad when you were seven, the memory of such innocent thrills is sure to make you smile larger than the sign of Uncle Fun himself. Old library card-filled drawers and cubby holes are stuffed with trinkets, so close your eyes and stick your hands inside to find prizes like rubber toy owls, superhero stickers and plastic gemmed rings.

1338 W Belmont
(773) 477.8223
Belmont

Hollywood Mirror

Resale and vintage fiends will find their Mecca at Hollywood Mirror. You can tell from looking at the display windows just what you're in for as you walk through the argyle styled doorway: '70s sun dresses, aprons, cowboy shirts, and tight jeans cover the mannequins and accessories such as mopeds, meat rugs and huge stuffed animals add some kitschy flare. Clothing and accessories for guys and gals pack the colorful store, as well as retro home accessories.

812 W Belmont
(773) 404.2044
Belmont

The Alley

Calling all bikers and badasses: Mega-metal haven The Alley carries everything you need for your next head-banging bash. You're slapped with the smell of leather when you walk in, as its heavy leather supply is showcased just up the front stairs. Venture into one of many rooms to find anarchic jewelry and belt buckles, a gallery of punk T-shirts, striped knee socks and torn fishnets and buckle-bound platform shoes. Complete your new metal makeover with a piercing or tattoo from the store's parlor.

858 W Belmont
(773) 525.3180
Belmont

Chicago Tattoo

46 Lakeview

Lakeview

Batteries Not Included

This is a one stop shop for any bachelorette party needs. You can find pretty much every crazy party accessory you could ever want, including candy panties, penis straws, blow up dolls, various oils and lotions, whips and feather boas. There is also a porn collection that will make anybody that passes by it blush. And with a name like Batteries Not Included, there is of course a wide variety of sex toys.

3420 N Halsted
(773) 935.9900
Belmont

Gaymart

This novelty store can be found in the heart of Boystown and features a variety of memorabilia from classic films and television shows. This shop is like an epicenter of pop culture that features everything from "Family Guy" action figures to "Wizard of Oz" clocks to life-size "Nightmare Before Christmas" dolls. There is also a large variety of pride flags, stickers and other accessories. You can also find a variety of gift cards, bags and wrapping paper.

3459 N Halsted
(773) 929.4272
Addison

Clothes Optional

This is one of the few places in Chicago that can be called a "Vintage Clothing and Art Boutique." While Clothes Optional is big on fun '70s and '80s vintage clothing, shoes and accessories, it also features paintings by local artists that are available to buy. The store is host to art shows about every two months. They have an incredible selection of clothing including prom dresses, scarves, T-shirts, belts, bell bottoms, clutch purses, boots, high heels and luggage.

2918 N Clark
(773) 296.6630
Diversey

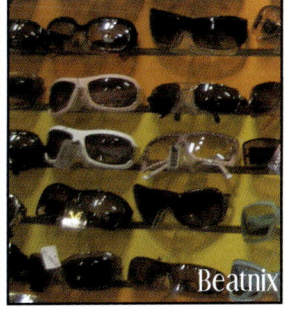

Ragstock

Tucked away from the streaming Belmont Avenue traffic, Ragstock is the perfect place to find something to add to an outfit or something crazy for a costume party. Everything from men's ties to suspenders, from women's skirts to thigh-high stocks, from hairy wigs to ridiculous sunglasses can be found in Ragstock. Watch for the photos of the clientele's dogs in the very front of the store.

812 W Belmont
(773) 868.9263
Belmont

Gramaphone

If you're looking for the latest vinyl in Chicago, this exclusively electronic record shop is the real deal with Chicago's audio addicts. Although Gramophone is driven by demand of Chicago's top DJs, the overall atmosphere is welcoming. An extensive collection of House is featured along with ample amounts of techno, electro and obscure '80s releases. You can preview your choices on one of the stores turntables. DJ supplies like needles and slip mats are offered too.

2663 N Clark
(773) 47.-3683
22 to Drummond

Land of the Lost

Remember when you were younger and you went over to your friend's house and it was full of board games, weird stitched wall fixtures, old records and clothes? Come into Land of the Lost, and even the smell of the place will bring you back to those days. Filled with old print tees, baseball T-shirts, cowboy boots and plaid shirts, they have a large variety of any type of vintage clothing you need.

614 W Belmont
(773) 529.4966
Belmont

Architectural Revolution

When a room needs something unusual to add a twist, look no further than Architectural Revolution. The large Belmont store has everything from beaded photo frames to Romanesque sculptures to spruce up any room. Unique postcards, bongo drums and incense are among the other unusual items tucked away in Architectural Revolution. If you need to revamp your own style, one portion of the store is dedicated to bohemian garb.

614 W Belmont
(773) 529.4966
Belmont

Beatnix

When it comes to outlandish clothing and accessories, Beatnix offers a taste of everything with a clientele to match. Patrons can find everything from casual T-shirts, cowboy boots, $5 designer sweaters to feather boas. The store caters to its Boystown patrons, displaying tiaras behind the counter and devoting one area to make-up and wigs. Even if you're not looking for drag wear, Beatnix has something for everyone: $2 VHS tapes, handcuffs, lunchboxes and other odd accessories.

3400 N Halsted
(773) 281.6933
Belmont

Silver Moon

Nestled in the heart of Halsted Street, this upscale store offers high-quality vintage clothing to those who are willing to pay for it. Furnished with decorative memorabilia, Silver Moon displays its ornate stock with artsy care. For men, fedoras, cummerbunds and bow ties could make any regular man a dapper fellow. For women, lacy lingerie, silky gowns and hats make any girl a lady. Even if prices are too high, this store makes for a nostalgic trip down dress-up lane.

3337 N. Halsted
(773) 883.0222
Belmont

Shane

If you like spending lots of money to look like you walked out of a thrift store, Shane is the place for you. Flimsy "vintage" Beatles and Blondie shirts sell for around $150, and torn and worn Tag jeans sell for about $200. Even tiny tie-dyed studded tanks for girls and every-color thermals for guys run $60. Surprisingly, Shane's sleek wooden shelves do house some rather affordable, trendy Cubs gear a la Urban Outfitters.

3657 N Southport
(773) 549.0179
Southport

Bookworks

Just a few blocks away from Wrigley Stadium, this used bookstore nestled into Addison Avenue seems out of place in one of Chicago's rowdiest areas. Walls are lined with shelves overflowing with books of all subjects. Each section is well-marked and books are easy to find despite their huge collections. Used CDs and records can be found in addition to the unusual selection of books. This bookshop is a nice escape from the usual boisterous Addison action.

3444 N Clark
(773) 871.5318
22 to Newport

Medusa's Circle

Beatnix

Elias

This Clark Street boutique offers unusual, trendy clothing at unusual, reasonable prices. A girl is not likely to buy a silky skirt or camisole that other girls will be wearing if she buys it at Elias. Aside from the store's petit collection of unique garments, a number of designed jewelry pieces are sold at Elias as well. The employees are eager to help their customers who often become regulars, seeing what is new in the store.

2919 N. Clark
(773) 477.5516
Wellington

Broadway Antique Market

Get lost in the maze of all that is retro. The vast Broadway Antique Market sells and rents out vintage findings from 75 different antique dealers. Artifacts from the 1933 Chicago World's Fair are on display, as well as '40s gold pumps, '50s bold plastic dinnerwear, and '60s Americana memorabilia. The price reflects items' great condition: a '70s cream and blue diamond coffee pot costs $35. At least take the time to admire the well-preserved past.

6130 N Broadway
(773) 743.5444
Granville

Wooden Spoon

If the Food Network seems like the only TV channel worth watching, put your viewing pleasure into practice with the help of Wooden Spoon. Stocked with the latest gadgets of the cooking world, from metal grilling tongs to bold-colored silicon bakeware, the Wooden Spoon specializes in gourmet kitchenware. You can even take one of four weekly cooking classes Wooden Spoon offers in its kitchen located in the back of the store.

5047 N Clark
(773) 293.3190
81 to Clark

Hubba Hubba

This upscale and very girly boutique has a shabby-chic décor that attracts all kinds of trendy young women. With local designers and well known brands like Michael Stars, this is the place to go in Lakeview to find the latest "in" styles. The shop also features a "girl's night out" shopping and cocktail party about every six weeks for customers and people on their mailing list.

3309 N Clark
(773) 477-1414
Belmont

Metal Haven

This record store truly lives up to its name. If you are not a true, hardcore

Lakeview 49

metal fan, you will feel slightly out of place here. Filled with black concert T-shirts, a huge variety of metal cads with an NC17 section, a vinyl selection, books, DVDs, and Ozzy Osbourne and Iron Maiden dolls, this is the place to go to get your metal fix.

604 Belmont
(773) 755.9202
Belmont

Windward Sports

If you want a one stop shop for all and any kind of extreme sport, definitely hit up Windward Sports and you will be sure to find everything you need. A knowledgeable employee will help you to find anything you need for surfing, skateboarding, snowboarding, in-line skating and windsurfing. Clothing and shoes for all of these sports are also available with brands like Billabong, Local Motion and Roxy.

3317 N Clark
(773) 472-6868
Belmont

Disgraceland

This laid-back resale shop features casual clothes for both men and women. Unlike most vintage shops, Disgraceland features a lot of name brand clothing with items from Abercrombie and Fitch, Banana Republic and Express and the clothes are only a few years old. Jackets, shoes, pants and skirts are all fairly cheap too. You can also find all kinds of accessories here as well, but, unlike the clothes, not all of them are name brand.

3338 N Clark
(773) 281.5875
Belmont

Yesterday

Full of old movie posters, baseball cards and comics, Yesterday is a small store full of old memories. Anything old and print will most likely be found here with stacks of old newspapers, magazines, books, single-page advertisements, pulp novels, postcards, records and even cereal boxes. You can also come in and sell back any of the previously listed items too, with the most popular item being, of course, baseball cards.

1143 W Addison
(773) 248.8087
Addison

LuLu's at the Belle Kay

This upscale vintage boutique that specializes in '50s style clothing, shoes and accessories is all about glamour. LuLu's is so glam that it was once mentioned in an episode of Sex and the City. Racks of beautiful dresses, furs, coats, purses, shoes, jewelry and hats that you will find at LuLu's will remind you of the pure joy that being a girl can bring. The items are in fabulous condition, and the price tag definitely matches the high quality.

3862 N. Lincoln
(773) 404.5858
Irving Park

Vintage Deluxe

If rockabilly is all your style, Vintage Deluxe is the place to go. The clothing is big on '50s, '60s and '70s styles, but what's most appealing is the costume jewelry, decade-old shoes and the large variety of '50s style glasses. You can also find vintage furniture, kitchenware and home décor in this stylish boutique. The high quality clothing is also made available at reasonable prices.

1846 W. Belmont
(773) 529.7008
Paulina

Panache

This small but sweet boutique offers a very girly and fun kind of fashion for women. Feminine skirts, dresses, tops and jewelry are offered among the local, national and international lines carried in Panache. Popular among college students and younger business women, Panache has a feel for what is young, hot and trendy in the fashion world.

2252 N Clark
(773) 477.4537
73 to Lincoln

Tragically Hip

If there could be only one word to describe the style of Tragically Hip, it would have to be hip, of course. As the name could indicate, the moderately priced clothing in Tragically Hip is constantly changing to keep up with the ever fickle fashions among the young and stylish. Locally designed jewelry is available here and the sales rack is full of unbelievable bargains.

931 W Belmont
(773) 549.1500
Belmont

Jive Monkey

Iron-on print tees are what this vintage clothing store is known for. Although its space is small, Jive Monkey contains a wide variety of vintage tees, blazers, dresses and even Boy Scout uniform shirts. The prices are very affordable and the quality is pretty high. And with a selection of new and vintage bracelets and bangles, you can come in and finally find the Bon Jovi slap bracelet you've always wanted.

854 W. Belmont
(773) 883.1800x229
Belmont

Yellow Jacket

Wonder where all the cool kids buy their digs? They go to Yellow Jacket. And with a convenient Lakeview location, Chicago kids can save some el fare and stop vintage-store-hopping to complete their look. Wearable vintage for guys and gals from past decades look crisp and clean, and prices are super reasonable. Luggage, shoes and accessories will also blow hipsters away.

2959 N Lincoln
(773) 248.1996
76 to Lakewood

Early to Bed

Looking for an intimate sex shop that won't make you feel awkward and dirty? Early to Bed is just the right place. Owned and run by women, you'll be sure to get personal attention on all of your intercourse inquires. Besides offering a wide range of dildos, vibrators, and other sex toys, hard to find vegan-friendly condoms and lube are also available.

5232 N Sheridan
(773) 271.1219
146 to Sheridan

Taboo Tabou

This erotic boutique features everything kinky you could imagine. The clothing, or lack thereof, at Taboo Tabou includes sexy underwear, lingerie, bathing suits and even some naughty latex items that might make you blush. Erotic novelties are also available to fulfill bachelorette party needs. There is also a wide variety of vibrators, dildos, lubes and condoms.

858 W Belmont
(773) 723.3739
Belmont

to play.

Beer, Wrigley Field, Munching, Midori Sour, Jukebox Picks, Zambrino, Apple Cider Bee

Cubby Bear

The Cubby Bear Lounge is conveniently located directly across from Wrigley Field where it has stood since 1953. With four rooms and five bars, there is ample room to accommodate the huge game day crowds. This newly renovated bar has been named one of the best sports bars in the area several times over. This includes Maxim's best neighborhood bar. Along with a wide choice of beers, you can also enjoy live on stage music Thursday, Friday and Saturday.

1059 Addison
(773) 327.1662
Addison

Berlin

Dance, Dance, Dance! Located in boystown, one can expect a very eye opening night at Berlin. The fantastic sound system and vivid visual displays will keep the energy going everyday of the week. If you are lucky you can make it to a theme night, such as the last Wednesday of every month's disco night. Although Berlin is a gay club its crowd seems to be very diverse. So if you like to dance, then you might not find a better place in Chicago.

3400 N Clark
(773) 528.4033
Belmont

Cherry Red

As one might assume Cherry Red, is well, red. Trying to be hip and chic, this establishment's red décor and lounge feel combine energy with a bit of comfort. You can dance on the weekends, or sit back and enjoy a moderately priced beverage. The mixed crowd adds something really nice to the atmosphere of this seemingly upscale night club.

2833 N Sheffield
(773) 477.3661
Diversey

Underground Lounge

If you're looking for an alternative to the sea of sports bars and chic ethnic foods on North Clark, then take a few steps down from Newport and into the hippest performance venue this side of The Metro. See local indie/folk stylings, such as City Electric and Bill Bungeroth or improvisational theater with groups such as The Sirens and The Franchise while having a drink at the bar in front of a couple flat-panel TVs showing the latest Sci-Fi space opera.

3855 N Lincoln
(773) 404.9494
Irving Park

Sheffield's

It's a bold move to bear to the street you're located on but Sheffield's pulls it off. Walking in, you feel like you're at the steps of a massive red wood converted into a bar. Inside is pure carved unity, with oak bars, walls and benches. Step outside and you're nestled right by the street, but with a warm sense of seclusion, tucked into a harmonic sanctuary of affordable drink specials and service adorned with

52 Lakeview

Lakeview

smiley wood nymphs pre-beer goggles.

3258 N Sheffield
(773) 281.4989
Belmont

Kit Kat Lounge

The Kit Kat lounge is a unique upscale martini bar with a '40s and '50s theme. The black and white films on multiple projectors, a themed menu and female celebrity impersonators throughout the night offer a unique dining experience. The menu includes aptly titled dishes such as the Top Hat Tender, Moulin Rouge, or the New York, New York. With an amazing selection of over 80 martinis and specials such as half off martinis every Tuesday and Sunday, this place shouldn't be missed.

3700 N Halsted
(773) 525.1111
Addison

Pepper Lounge

The Pepper Lounge is an art-nouveau exercise in red velvety interior design with a magical forest as a backyard. Take a night out at the P Lounge and you'll be whisked away to a trippy style blending your journey to 1950s Chicago and the backrooms of Alice in Wonderland. Dress fancy. And buy martinis. Buy many martinis.

3441 Sheffield
(773) 665.7377
Addison

Hi-Tops

Prepare to be bombarded with sport at Hi-Tops. It's inescapable, with 65 screens jam packed into this two story establishment. You can enjoy your favorite sporting event while munching on the above average selection of bar food or bring yourself out on Wednesday nights for Karaoke. So check this place out before, during, or after the game for spectacular sports coverage.

3551 Sheffield
(773) 348.0009
Addison

Elbo Room

This prominent music venue in Chicago doesn't disappoint. You can enjoy the fun atmosphere and the college music loving crowd in the basement or you can enjoy a drink upstairs in the comfortable seating. The music seeker will appreciate the great sound that comes from very capable PA engineers, while the casual patron will enjoy an above average selection of beers, and a jukebox upstairs.

2871 N. Lincoln
(773) 549.5549
Diversey

Spin

This primarily gay, lesbian, and bisexual dance club features a popular Friday night shower contest. Contestants get down and clean in this weekly contest. The sounds you'll hear from this place are techno/disco, as well as live music in the backroom. If the shower contest doesn't win you over the decently priced drinks and the free pizza Monday nights just might.

800 W Belmont
(773) 327.7711
Belmont

Duke of Perth

If you want to find a bar that has good foreign beer, home style foods and deer heads on the wall, Duke of Perth is for you. This Scottish themed bar and restaurant is popular for its authentic Scottish drinks, including their very popular apple cider beer. On Mondays you can buy one entrée and get the next for half price and all day Thursday you can get a pint for $3.50.

2913 N Clark
(773) 477.1741
Wellington

Lincoln Park

to shop:
 Out of the west, Paul Frank

lincoln park

To eat:
 Tillies, Annette's Ice, Vosges

to play:
 Beat Kitchen, The Apartment

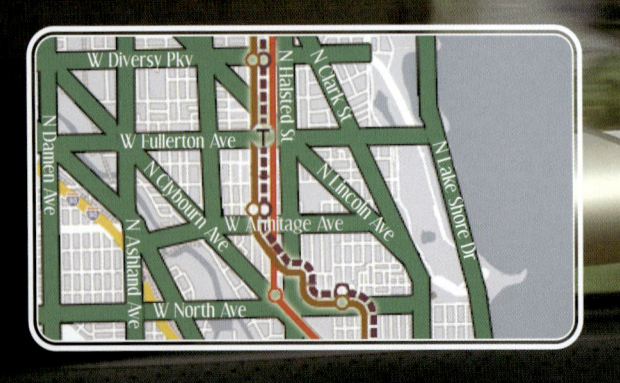

54 Chicago Unzipped

Unzipped

Everywhere you want to be...

As the city "just north of the real scene," the historical Lincoln Park really holds its own weight in the Chicagoland area. With the Lincoln Park campus of DePaul University in the area, Lincoln Park caters to every crowd. There are places for the emo, goth, prep, classy, sophisticated and the downright wild. But besides having a place for whatever your fancy, Lincoln Park boasts beautiful parks, an expansive lake shore and of course, the completely free Lincoln Park Zoo, home of 1200 animals.

While this town maintains an upscale aura, the town is receptive to every person around: aside from the beauty of the town and the wide array of fun places to eat and shop, Lincoln Park residents are more than ready to tell you their favorite spot, or even where those elusive elephants are in the zoo. On top of that, this town has the usual spattering of bars, dance clubs and all-night coffee houses. The architecture in many parts of town has remained the same since the late 1800s, making this city one of the most culturally-rich in all of Chicago. Lincoln Park may not be a jumping spot 24/7, but it's a beautiful break from the bustling city.

lincoln park.

to eat.

Tea, Asiago Cheese, Peach Italian Ice, Hogies with the works, Elk Snack Sticks, Pickle

The Bourgeois Pig

If this were 1923, the Bourgeois Pig would resemble your grandmother's kitchen or the town general store (think tin pots and wooden tables). Laid back, quiet and dimly lit, this coffee house serves up strong brew and also offers various panini and soup options. The second floor features pieces of art and, when the weather is nice, seating is available outside. Swing by on a Friday or Saturday and you may hear live music.

738 W. Fullerton
(773) 883.5282
Fullerton

Annette's Homemade Italian Ice

This sidewalk sorbet stand serves 13 different flavors of their signature Italian ice. The discerning patron can choose between tall cups of frosted lime, mango, passion fruit and others, sometimes with tiny chunks of fruit mixed in. For those who favor tradition, Annette's also offers ice cream. Take your cone over to one of the nearby picnic tables and remember the bygone days of grade school summers. Verdict: Sweet and satisfying.

2105 W. Armitage
(773) 772.5349
Bus: 50 to Armitage

Twisted Lizard

The fiesta experience at Twisted Lizard is so intense that it has to be below street level. Those who risk the steep climb down to the restaurant's subterranean red quarters will discover that this joint has it all: string lights shaped like chili peppers, furniture fashioned from tree trunks, and tostadas topped with slices of cactus. The food is fantastic and the complimentary salsa is a great addition to any cuisine. For those over 21, the restaurant turns into a dance bar at night.

1964 N. Sheffield
(773) 929.1414
Armitage

Ambrosia Café

Ambrosia Café has two faces. It offers coffee and sandwiches during the day, but at night it becomes a smoky hookah lounge. Lattes are lean and mean, but the décor truly leaves onlookers breathless. The plum and pumpkin colored walls make the café a chic afternoon pit stop, but trendy black couches turn it into a den of mystery. Which will it be? As the guest you can choose, but do so quickly-this multifaceted phantom goes to bed at 1 a.m.

1963 N. Sheffield
(773) 404.4450
9 to Sheffield

Twisted Lizard

56 Lincoln Park

Lincoln Park

Chicago Bagel Authority

At CBA, patrons choose from a list of at least 50 options and combine ingredients as diverse as horseradish, muenster, and avocado to create their own innovative steamed bagel sandwiches. Choose side dishes of bananas, cereal, and other snacks. Special cooking directions cost an extra 25 cents, but you wouldn't want these yummy subs any other way. Plus, win one of their monthly contests and you'll end up eating free.

953 W. Armitage
(773) 248.9606
8 to Armitage

Shine/Morida Restaurant

There's no real door into Shine/Morida. Instead, floor-to-ceiling windows swing open all along the restaurant's façade, literally inviting patrons in off the street. Step in and you'll notice the clean white furniture and soothing blue and green décor contrast with crisp, flavorful Japanese/Chinese cuisine. The seafood is pricey, but the rest of the menu is reasonable.

901 W. Armitage
(773) 296.0101
Armitage

Pasta Palazzo

Pasta Palazzo is that rarest of eateries: a place where the "healthy" menu options are delicious and the "regular" menu options aren't that bad for your health. The specialty tortellini and gnocchi are great. Or try one of the no-cheese, no-fat "healthy options" - the ingredients are all fresh and grilled separately. Just hit up the ATM before you dine, because the restaurant only accepts payment in cash.

1966 N. Halsted
(773) 248.1400
Armitage

Gepperth's Meat Market

Ham, turkey, beef…elk snack sticks? Whether planning an outdoor barbecue or a private steak dinner,

Vosges: Vosges provides the proverbial chocolate orgasm in slab, truffle, or powdered form. This purple-painted, glass-chandeliered shrine to chocolate sells a variety of smooth, traditional flavors in colorful foil chocolate boxes. Those in search of culinary adventure should try the signature "exotic" truffles, which mix chocolate with wasabi, ginger, and curry spice. Kitchen scientist extraordinaire Katrina whips up a new batch every month. Watch out for the prices, though: at Vosges, "haut chocolat" reigns supreme. **2105 W Armitage** (773) 772.5349

Gepperth's will probably be able to pair you with a meat to match your occasion. The business has been operating in Lincoln Park for over 50 years, and in addition to meat, they also sell all types of barbecue and grill sauces. For those who can't be bothered to cook, try the frozen pre-packaged section, with everything from sausage to shrimp bowls.

1964 N. Halsted
(773) 549.3883
8 to Armitage

Giselle's

Giselle is a supermodel's name, and Giselle's is the sort of food boutique supermodels would patronize - if

Lincoln Park 57

they ate. Nonetheless, their loss is the customer's gain at this lovely cottage-styled eatery with elegant crackers, wines, and cheeses. The prepared foods feature ingredients like orzo, feta, and sliced tuna, all for prices pretty much equal to what you'd get at Whole Foods. They even have free wine and cheese tasting on select weekends.

1967 N. Halsted
(312) 266.7880
8 to Armitage

Tin Tin

Tin Tin's electric lime and orange walls match the cheery mood that ice cream delivers to its eaters. Sit with a cup or cone of ice cream and watch the staffers' kids run around the store with paper airplanes and tall cups of bubble tea. All the ice cream flavors taste good, but if you're looking for something a little different, try Chinese Green Tea or After Dinner Mint (vanilla with crushed up mint candy).

2468 N. Clark
(773) 549.1715
22 to Roslyn

Zig Zag

This modern American-Italian kitchen prides itself on quality dishes with fresh ingredients. But with plates like chicken ficotta, fettuccini and BBQ chicken salads, you wonder why this restaurant that seats only about 30 doesn't reach max capacity. The answer is Zig Zag caters its delicious dishes to parties of six or more. Every item can be shipped out for your dining pleasure with-

in a 100 mile radius from its cozy location.

2436 N Lincoln
(773) 344.2222
Fullerton

Red Lion Pub

The Red Lion Pub is an authentic English getaway for those itching for British cuisine and cozy pub atmosphere. Hearty traditional British dishes like beans on toast, bangers and mash, Welsh rarebit and Cornish pastries flood the menu and fill the stomachs of a large number of regulars who stay for a pint at the ornately decorated pub. But be careful on the second floor party room overlooking the spacious beer garden: it's haunted!

2446 N Lincoln
(773) 348.2695
Fullerton

Original Chicago Hoagie Hut

OK, so this is not the original Hoagie Hut, you'd have to venture out to Highwood, Ill. to find #1. But because this location wasn't the first doesn't mean their hoagies are second best. Stuffed with cheese, sirloin, lettuce, tomato, mayo, American cheese, spices and oil, and at about $6 a pop, you just can't go wrong. If you're not up for a hoagie that's greasy, cheesy and messy, you can always

The Wiener's Circle: It ain't pretty, but the Wiener's Circle gets the job done. In this shack, with black and red linoleum floors and purple vinyl stools, order up a Vienna beef hot dog (steamed or charred) and some fries. If it's hot, eat at one of the outdoor picnic tables. The service is brusque but gets it right. Ask for the works - hot peppers, pickles, tomatoes, mustard, raw or grilled onions, and relish. The perfect Chicago dog. **2622 N. Clark** (773) 477.7444
Bus: 22, 36 to Drummond Pl; 76 to Broadway/Clark

fall back on a burger, hot dog or a number of sides.

2580 N Lincoln
(773) 248.0900
Fullerton

Noodles in the Pot

Noodles in the Pot boasts that it serves "Thai noodles at its best" and it's true. Noodles in the Pot is where to go if you're looking for perfectly cooked Pad Thai. Head over if you like cheap (under $6) lunch specials, eating with elderly Thai couples, people-watching DePaul students, or if you just need somewhere that's BYOB. In nice weather, one entire wall lifts up, doubling the size of the restaurant with tables added in the adjacent alley.

2453 N. Halsted
(773) 975.6177
Fullerton

Argo Tea

This cheeky Armitage Avenue café sits right across the street from a Starbucks. All types of locals gather at Argo for bright décor, spicy chai and free wireless internet. The staff isn't strict about kicking people out, which makes Argo a great spot to study or just to pick up a coffee. One thing to watch out for: patrons are expected to share the space with an enormous collection of decorative pastel teapots.

958 W. Armitage
(773) 388.1880
Armitage

Simply Soup Co.

Have you been dreaming of a healthy and unique "fast food" restaurant that specializes in soup? Dream no more! Simply Soup Co. is open for business. Choose from a rotating menu of 12 freshly made specialty soups to fill your craving, like Saucy Sicilian Pizza, sweet and creamy Chicken Almond, light and fruity Chilled Raspberry and Yogurt and oddly popular Dill Pickle. The café also serves coffee, espresso and gelato.

2142 N Halsted
(773) 871.7687
8 to Webster

R.J. Grunts

R.J. Grunts is a comfortable hub for casual American fare. With heavy wooden booths and décor authentic from their early days in the '70s. Check out framed black and white portraits of the stylish locals from that era that fill the back wall. Grunts can offer nostalgia to those looking for their share of Americana. Besides a great menu of shakes, malts and floats, their famous 50+ ingredient all-you-can-eat soup and salad bar is well worth the $11.

2056 N Lincoln
(773) 929.5363
36 to Clark

Nookies Too

How many diners include a wait staff of young, good-looking English speakers? At Nookies Too, the second of two Nookies locations, enjoy not only attractive and friendly service, but classic diner dishes like a solid cheeseburger. Keep an eye out for the soup of the day and the apple crepes; both are typically worth ordering. Nookies Too is a good choice when you're looking for a great diner experience.

2112 N Halsted
(773) 327.1400
8 to Dickens

Lincoln Park

to shop.

's Moving Castle, Daisy Petals, Howdy, Inner Bitch, Bangles, Hipster, Limited Release, K

Chicago Costume Co., Inc.

Want a standout Easter Bunny suit, stage makeup, or Mardi Gras beads? Look no further than Chicago Costume. The friendly staff will gladly rent you a costume or sell you a prepackaged one (our favorites include the naughty detective and the belly dancer). Whatever you're in the market for, you're sure to find it hanging from the walls, be it sunglasses or fake teeth. A destination shop, even if you're just in the mood to browse.

1120 W. Fullerton
(773) 528.1264
Fullerton

Odd Obsession Movies

Organized by director and theme and categorized into sections like Euro-trash Sleaze (films include Caligula II and Salon Kitty) and Japanese Classics (shelves marked Akira Kurosawa and Sexy Tough Girls), the film selection can't be beat at this basement-level indie rental shop. Membership is free and three-day rentals are cheap at Odd Obsession, where most films are available on DVD, but some VHS tapes still sit on the red and green shelves. Movie buff? This place is for you.

1659 N. Halsted
(312) 573.9910
North/Clybourn

Tribeca

The owner of this colorful boutique stocks the store with her favorite designers and trends. The ruffles and chiffon are fun to flip through, but what makes Tribeca a great experience is the ambiance. The sunny boutique has strawberry-painted walls and floor-length mirrors. There's a white wicker couch and magazines so your friends won't get bored while you shop. Although the friendly fashion advice is free, the clothes are very pricey. You'll want to bring Mom along to pay.

1013 W. Armitage
(773) 296.2997
Armitage

Out of the West

The sign outside the horse-stall doors of this Western-style boutique reads, "We know our denim." You will too, since the designer brands in this store are the same ones you'd find anywhere on Michigan Avenue. But here, western paraphernalia reigns supreme. The rope-wrapped entryway and scrubbed wood floors will make you want to grab a pair of cowboy boots and try your hand at rodeo. But watch out: although the décor screams Texas, the prices are pure Lincoln Park.

1000 W. Armitage
(773) 404.9378
Armitage

Buy Popular Demand

Looking for trendy handbags, Juicy jeans and Michael Stars shirts at a fraction of the price? Search the packed racks of clothing at this consignment shop for amazing finds, usually under $20. Some of the clothing is a bit librarian-oriented, like chunky sweaters and print blouses, but a lot of it is very much in fashion. Except for the inexpensive designer shoes, which are rather worn in, most things for sale look like they've never been touched.

2629 N. Halsted
(773) 868.0404
8 to Wrightwood

Lincoln Park

Stilettos, Mermaid, Chunky, Haute, Earth-toned, L

Ame

Any establishment that calls itself "a sanctuary for the senses" has to smell like incense and Ame is no exception. The bottom floor is stocked with herbal lotions for every part of the human body. The three-floor spa offers treatments such as "Rain Drop Therapy" and "Couples Massage." The experience might be worth the price since the spa packages come with lunches and a calming ambiance. Ame's in-house team of designers create a collection of earth-toned clothing every season.

1006 W. Armitage
(773) 929.4999
Armitage

Paper Source

Some people love movies. Some people love sports. Some people love paper. Like most passions, this one can't be easily explained. Some browse the witty collection of gift books and leave with a copy of "The Action Heroine's Guide," while others nearly expire from sensory overload from racks of colorful textured papers. The pre-cut cards, ribbons, and stamps are worth a stop, but repeat customers are mainly "serial scrap-bookers."

919 W. Armitage
(773) 525.7300
Armitage

Original Expressions

Unlike the many "card stores" that also sell pens, tableware, party supplies and other gizmos, Original Expressions sticks to stationery. Though all the cards are cute and artsy, the best are the "humorous" cards. Most humorous cards are painfully lame, but the ones at Original Expressions are actually entertaining. The collection of "inner bitch" books is also worth a glance, if only to see where you fall on the "inner bitch" spectrum.

845 W. Armitage
(773) 975.2010
Armitage

Art Effect

This massive store, organized into sections like clothing and kitchenware, sells everything a hipster girl needs, from long, brightly beaded necklaces ($20) to a three piece polka-dot martini set ($29). Some items, like delicate leather coin purses, are pricey, but the huge selection of everything from travel books to sun hats, displayed on racks, hooks and shelves, ensures something for everyone. The friendly staff will help you explore while jazzy Spanish music plays throughout the store.

934 W. Armitage
(773) 929.3600
Armitage

Ancient Echoes

If you have a silver fetish, you will go nuts in Ancient Echoes, but the store can attract plenty of others. Jewelry in the outer room ranges from gorgeous to tasteless, but with much more character than anything found at Tiffany's. The curtained backrooms are furnished with thick Persian rugs, dim red lights and sequined Indian-style cushions. The store's chimes that cling in the background suggest a foreign boudoir more than just a trendy shop.

1022 W. Armitage
(773) 880.1003
Armitage

Cynthia Rowley

Although the decoration at this boutique (featuring several upside-down umbrellas) doesn't always make sense, the long walls set off racks of brightly embroidered cocktail dresses. The décor doesn't discourage faithful shoppers from coming back and browsing the extensive collection. There are shirts and pants mixed into the sparse collection, but at Rowley's prices you might want to save this store for special occasion shopping. Besides, the dresses are lovely.

808 W. Armitage
(773) 528.6160
Armitage

Fischers Flowers

A tropical garden blooms inside this florist's plain front door. Fresh, brilliant flowers in all shapes and shades lend the air a sweet fragrance. Prices for traditional plants like roses and daisies are much lower at Fischers than at most boutique "flower shoppes." The store also sells shaped vases with splashy orange, blue, and green patterns worked into the flowing glass.

852 W. Armitage
(773) 248.1900
Armitage

Sage

The jewelry at Sage is both delicate and eye-catching. Some items include thin chokers of silver and pearls, teardrop earrings made of blazing aqua stones, curling glass necklaces. The hand-dyed silk scarves come in a variety of subtle shades. This isn't the place to play dress-up: the jewelry is real silver and semi-precious stones, and prices start around $25. But if you're looking for something genuine to match your cocktail dress, Sage is one of the best places to look.

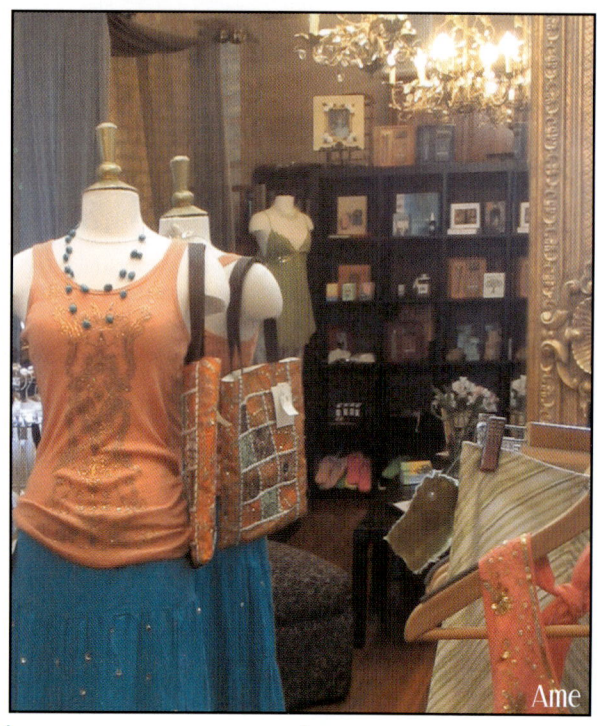

843 W. Armitage
(773) 388.3300
Armitage

McShane's Exchange

"If you can't afford your own designer wardrobe, buy someone else's," read the signs at McShane's Exchange. Problem is, at $200 for a consignment Armani jacket (some would consider this a steal) the phrase might be better as "if you can't afford your own designer wardrobe, buy nothing at all." Nonetheless, there are some genuinely amazing bargains in the clearance section upstairs. Just make sure to check zippers and sleeves: some of these clothes have been more than "gently" used.

815 W. Armitage
(773) 525.0282
Armitage

My Masala

Indian-inspired clothing and artistic jewelry make My Masala stand out from the average boutique. Jeans, tank tops and sweatshirts line the store, but with surprisingly placed slits and patterns, they are not the usual trendy shop fare. Beaded slippers, throw pillows and loose shirts add the Indian flavor to My Masala, and the table of jewelry in the center of the store makes the shop memorable. Highlights include sparkling cocktail rings ($24) and beaded wire bracelets ($48).

2574 Lincoln
(773) 327.0189
Fullerton

Mi Sun

Why is this long, narrow boutique not the most popular store on North Clark? Filled with floral and striped a-line skirts, metallic and leather shoulder bags, bone bracelets, fat beaded necklaces and bug-like sunglasses, Mi Sun carries just about everything you need to be a fabulous hipster. Mi Sun's friendly staff is a high point. Just don't breath too deep around the incense - you wouldn't want to sneeze on the jewelry case in the back.

2657 N. Clark
(773) 883.2024
36 to Clark

M. Boutique

This trendy jewelry and handbag boutique fits right in with Lincoln Park's chic style, but stands out when it comes to price tags. Unlike most exclusive shops, M. Boutique prices are very reasonable for how fashion-forward shoppers end up looking after a purchase. Purses are placed on tables and hung in bureaus that are flooded with chunky wooden beads, smooth shiny pearls, huge copper earrings and shiny bangle bracelets. Girls of all fashions are sure to find a favorite piece.

711 W. Armitage
(312) 397.1390
Armitage

Lush

Is it a candy store? Pyramids of orange rounds. Bowls of chocolate and blueberry pastes. Loaves of chunky avocado and citrus compotes. But the customer who bites into one of these products is in for a surprise - they're cosmetics. From creamy moisturizer bars to thick face masks to powdery "Hot Sex" bath bombs, Lush sells every conceivable bath supply. Unfortunately, like luxury foods, many Lush products are priced by the pound - and in Lush, it's all too easy to pack on the pounds.

859 W. Armitage
(773) 281.5874
Armitage

All She Wrote

Forget E-vites. Go to All She Wrote and create old-fashioned paper invitations for that big bash. Invites can be custom made for anything from turning 21 to costume parties on paper to match the feel of the night. Polka dots, Victorian landscapes, abstract shapes, and cute caricatures are only a few of the design choices. Even get your initials monogrammed on bags, bathrobes or, of course, cards. Browse through their collection of candles and other trinkets for fancy favors.

825 W. Armitage
(773) 529.0100
Armitage

Jane Hamill

If Jackson Pollock were to marry a wealthy French fashionista, their children might wear clothes from Jane Hamill's. Bright colors reign supreme in this store stocked with women's silk and satin formal dresses. Cutout daisies, splashes of colorful paint and chic trends mark the collection. The shop boasts more than high prices and low necklines: they also carry a large bridesmaid collection. Just be prepared to wait three months for the Cinderella magic to work: these bridesmaid gowns are specially ordered.

1117 W. Armitage
(773) 665.1102
Armitage

Lincoln Park 63

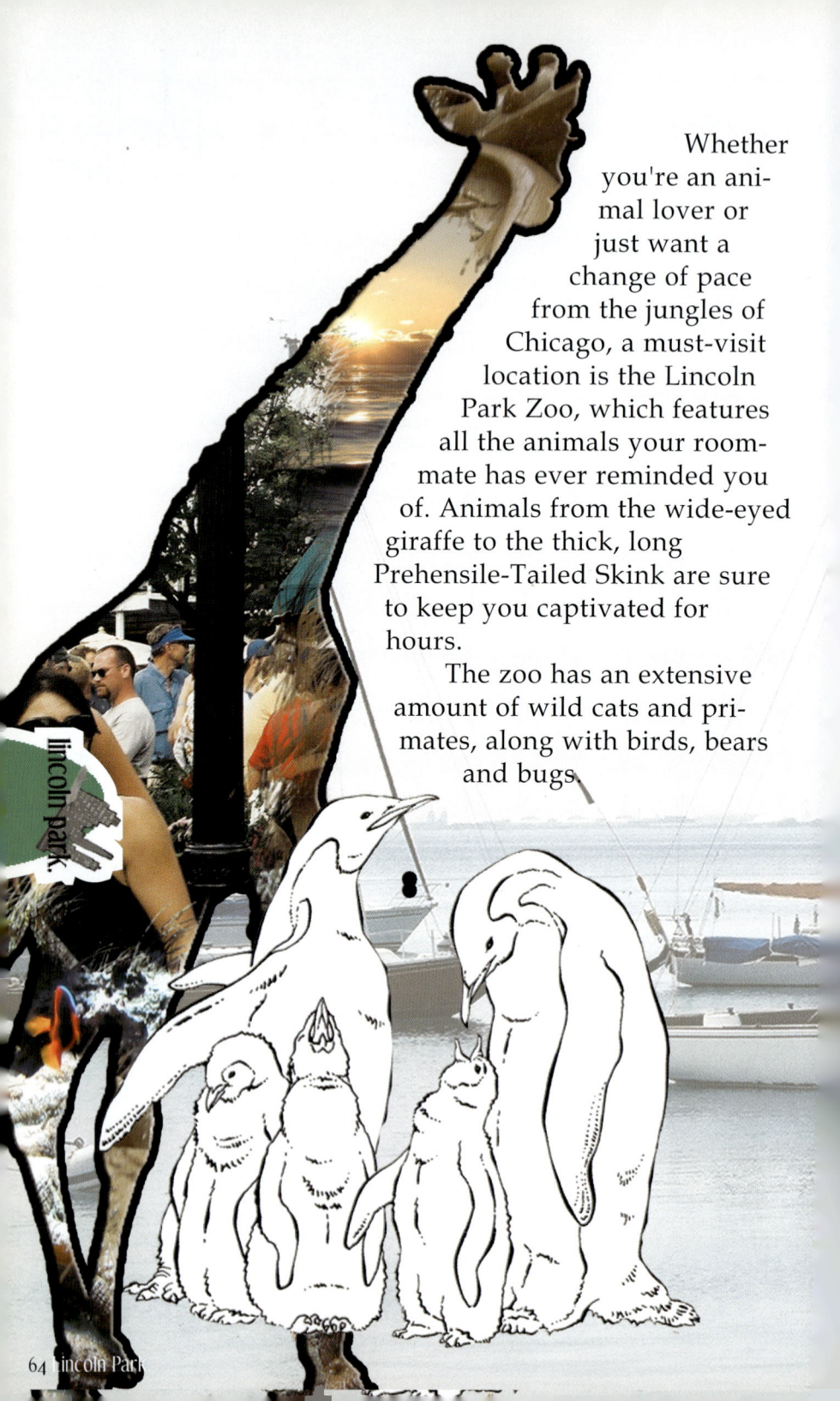

lincoln park.

Whether you're an animal lover or just want a change of pace from the jungles of Chicago, a must-visit location is the Lincoln Park Zoo, which features all the animals your roommate has ever reminded you of. Animals from the wide-eyed giraffe to the thick, long Prehensile-Tailed Skink are sure to keep you captivated for hours.

The zoo has an extensive amount of wild cats and primates, along with birds, bears and bugs.

Lincoln Park Zoo

Highlights include mini-windows in the rather smelly Small Mammal and Reptile House, where you can see infant Dwarf Mongooses, as well as the outdoor cat cages that house killer felines.

  The zoo has free admission, making it a popular destination for all walks of life around Chicago. No one can deny the appeal of animals from exotic places, easily making you forget that you're in the hub of a major city. The shows are all fun and enjoyable (you know seals doing tricks is just awesome).

  The zoo often offers educational lessons and special events, such as ZooLights during the winter season, when the zoo is open at night and millions of little lights are hung up to create a magical animal experience. All in all, you're never too old for the zoo.

to play.

Feel, Alternative Country, Beat Salad, Thai Pizza, Red Stripe, Industry Night, Tan Lines.

to try something else.

Beat Kitchen

This bar/music venue, while considerably out of the way, proves to be a hip and an all-around enjoyable experience. The music and bar portions of the club are segregated, so if you don't feel like watching whatever local band is going at it that night, you can chill in the small but homey outer bar, relax in one of the booths or watch a sporting event at the bar. There are many regulars, giving the Beat Kitchen a sort of neighborhood feel.

2100 Belmont
(773) 281.4444
Washington

Park West

A swanky music club for its swanky Lincoln Park location, Park West is a venue that will impress any concertgoer. A refreshing change from the grimy, paint-chipping-off-the-walls, floor-sticky-with-beer live music halls, Park West can hold up to 900 people in its five-tiered theater complete with numerous bars and black vinyl booths (usually reserved to walk-in's dismay) that surround the large dance floor. The stage caters to an eclectic range of artists-from comedy shows to jazz to rock-and patrons vary according to show.

322 W. Armitage
(773) 929.1322
22 to Armitage

to bar hop.

Wise Fools Pub

Wise Fools is a bit off the radar in terms of cool places to see live music in Chicago. That said, every once in a while a great act finds its way to the stage and some bands have been known to draw large crowds to this little bar in the heart of Lincoln Park. On an average night though, the bar is pretty low-key. It's a good place to unwind, giving patrons a refreshing change of pace from the trendy, yuppie-infested hang outs.

2270 N. Lincoln
(773) 929.1300
Fullerton

The Grand Central

Though The Grand Central houses 14 flat screens showcasing sports games, it is not a sports bar and grill-it's a classy local tavern. The menu includes high-end bar fare, such as chicken jumbo and sirloin burgers, and typical bar décor is given a posh twist: stained glass lanterns hang over large booths, and elegant colored light is thrown at brick walls. Experience live music from piano crooners to hoppin' DJs Thursday through Saturday.

950 W. Wrightwood
(773) 832.4000
Fullerton

Bordo's Eatery and Sauce

Bordo's offers Italian-American fusion cuisine with a hip edge. Orange and red velvet curtains drape over dark wooden windows looking into the posh front bar. The spacious back room works as the dining area where a number of pasta dishes as well as the popular Bordo Burger are served. The eatery's orange entrance is converted into a classy lounge where young professionals flock to one of Bordo's two long wooden bars to sip a drink from their 17-long martini madness list.

2476 N. Lincoln
(773) 529.6900
Fullerton

Yuppie-Punk Bar, Swanky, # Lincoln Park, Sonic Boom, The Game

to bar hop.

Blu

Blu is a perfect example of the slick and trendy side of Chicago nightlife. From the steep cover charges, to the steeper drink prices, you can easily find yourself dropping a significant amount of bill in this joint. Admittedly, the cheesy dance floor with its flashing strobes and light-up tiles can be pretty amazing while you're slurring song lyrics and the lofted upstairs lounge can provide the key atmosphere to chillax (read: chill and relax) with that special someone you met just five minutes ago.

2247 Lincoln
(773) 549.5884
Fullerton

The Apartment

Lincoln Park 67

Bucktown & Wicker Park

bucktown wicker park

to eat:
Earwax, Sweet Thang, Filter

to shop:
Shebang, Daffodil Hill, Myopic Books, Hot Pink

to play:
Nick's Beer Gardens, The Double Door

Unzipped

Old World hipsters...

Any place named by Polish settlers who had a lot of goats (males are called bucks) is bound to be an eclectic and fun place. Wicker Park and Bucktown certainly hold that thriving yet welcoming Chicago feel. These neighborhoods act as a cultural and ethnic hub within Chicago, as they are the home to many Poles, Germans and Scandinavians. The cobblestone alleys, the "Flat Iron Building," and buildings with beautiful stained glass add to the class of these historically-rich areas. But don't think that these neighborhoods are stuck in the past.

Wicker Park and Bucktown are two of the most quickly growing areas, with each street bursting with stores, bars, boutiques, restaurants and pretty much everything any hipster can desire. Boasting some of the most unique establishments in the entire Chicagoland area, these neighborhoods have a very distinct atmosphere: The people here are frequently more than happy to stop for a chat, even if their Slavic banter or hipster lingo makes no sense to you. Visitors often overlook these neighborhoods, but it is one of the few places that absolutely no one should miss. The culturally rich and edgy urban environment just adds to a fun experience of shopping and eating at some of the best-rated places in all of Chicago. And hey, you might learn something new while you're down there, even a new language.

bucktown
wicker park

www.ChicagoUnzipped.com

to eat.

El Gusto Taqueria Y Restaurante

If the local clientele of Taqueria Y Restaurante includes nurses on their lunch breaks, consider this an indication of a safe bet for authentic Mexican food. Though it may not be considered Chicago's best Mexican food, the quaintness of the family-run atmosphere and sit-down service isn't something you can find at your local Chipotle. The service is friendly and fast, and you can get a burrito meal, including refills of delicious tortilla chips with spicy green salsa, for under $6.

1408 N. Milwaukee
(773) 276.8670
Division

Sweet Thang

You don't have to see the photo of former President Bill Clinton pictured with the owner of this pastry shop to know that Sweet Thang is something special. It could be the old-school atmosphere, with fraying wall-paper and battered heart-shaped chairs. It could be award-winning Chef Bernard Runo and his array of croissants, quiches, quick breads and mousses with flavors from chocolate and key lime to mango and coconut pineapple. Whatever it is, Sweet Thang has many delights and charms to offer.

1921 W. North
(773) 772.4166
Damen

Piece

At Piece you come for the pizza, beer and the fact that cast members from "The Real World: Chicago" worked here during their stay in the Windy City. The naturally-lit, warehouse joint makes their specialty pizza without traditional mozzarella cheese, focusing on the ingredients in the sauce and toppings. More traditional pies are also popular. A medium pizza easily serves two or three, but this isn't Chicago deep-dish-multiple slices are easily consumed in one sitting.

1927 W. North
(773) 772.4422
Damen

Filter

With more square tables than needed for a giant game of checkers, this café is the Mecca for Bucktown's mobile and modern. A bastion of laptops and hair dye, the large spaces serve as outlets for anything: chatting on couches, examining art portfolios or munching on clever

70 Bucktown & Wicker Park

Bucktown & Wicker Park

menu items. Interesting selections include the tofu reuben, sweet potato fries and blueberry pomegranate smoothie, all offered for relatively reasonable prices by a large and cordial staff.

1585 N. Milwaukee
(773) 227.4850
Damen

Half and Half

For a quick pick-me-up drink in a coffee-shop half the size of a normal java joint, be sure to check out Half and Half. Lime green walls and black tables make this tiny establishment a cozy place to pick up simple coffee, smoothies or even gelato. But save the gelato for a particularly nice day where you can sit out on the sidewalk under their umbrellas while enjoying their seasonable menu, all with the soothing sounds of the el in the background.

1560 N. Damen
(773) 489.6220
Damen

Northside Bar & Grill

Girlfriend wants a date and you would like to pretend like you're listening to her while you watch the big game....perfect place. With an outdoor patio, a beergarden with sunroof and a back room complete with a big screen TV, cheer on the Cubs while chomping on the signature barbecue chicken sandwich. The beer, wine and cocktail selection is extensive and the food is reasonably priced. Expect to wait 15-20 minutes for a table, especially on game days.

1635 Damen
(773) 384.3555
Damen

Earwax Café: As if the Earwax Café's eccentric name and extensive menu of varied Mexican and traditional American fare weren't enough, the venue is dual-purpose: it also features a unique video rental gallery in its basement. The café houses multiple aisles of foreign and independent titles as well as shoeboxes of flattened and laminated VHS cases (redeemable with the actual video upon rental) labeled into categories such as "Horror," "Cult," and "Sci-Fi." There are some titles like "There's Something About Mary" but there's something about the Earwax Café that makes guests want to try a new movie genre.
1561 N. Milwaukee, (773) 772.4019, Damen

Babylon Eatery

Don't let the modest size of Babylon Eatery lead you to believe that the same adjective can describe the taste and flavor of its Middle Eastern cuisine. Shish kebabs, babba ghanoush, and falafel are more typical items found on its menu, but go all out and try more unusual dishes for an American pallet like pan fried beef or chicken in a curry paprika. Try a number of traditional Middle Eastern sweets after your main course in the orange eatery, or stay later when Babylon draws a diverse crowd for a weekend hookah lounge after 10 p.m. BYOB.

2023 N. Damen
(773) 278.1788
50 to Armitage

Green Ginger

With a popular Dim Sum brunch every Saturday and Sunday (think Chinese tapas) Green Ginger is a definite hot spot. Specializing in Pan-Asian seafood based cuisine, Green Ginger draws a hungry neighborhood crowd and fills them up with dishes such as the Macadamia Halibut with a side of mango chutney. The mint green walls and sleek wooden tables make for a relaxing atmosphere, especially for their $6-8 rice and noodle lunch specials.

2050 W. Division
(773) 486.6700
70 to Damen

Picante Taqueria

Be careful or you might pass by this hole-in-the-wall Mexican joint, but good food for great prices hide in this tiny yellow take-out place. While the most expensive item on the menu is steak fajitas for $9, you'll have no problem spending a little extra on horchata, sweet rice water, and Jarritos Mexican soda. Burritos stuffed with refried and black beans are huge, but if that's too much for you, there's no shame in getting the white boy taco. OK, well maybe a little.

2016 W. Division
(773) 328.8800
40 to Division

Cooking Fools

The whisks that line the walls of Cooking Fools let you know that they mean business. Fronting as a take-out for a catering company of the same name, Cooking Fools sells health-conscious prepared food that's also vegan friendly. Create your own gourmet dinner from a la cart choices of fish, meat or vegetable plates all made from scratch. For a quick stop-and-shop, grab a $4 lunch special or one of Cooking Fools' ice creams, sorbets or desserts, like the all-natural strawberry soy ginger popsicle.

1916 W. North
(773) 276.5565
Damen

Jinx

This ultra hip café draws mostly scenesters, so if you don't have tattoos or black rimmed glasses you might feel a bit unwelcome in Jinx. But those who can take the stare-down from customers and staff as you walk in the door will be pleasantly surprised at the collection of hot and cold drinks and light sandwiches. With chipping yellow and red painted walls, old coffee can light fixtures and furniture that even the Salvation Army would turn away, Jinx does have an edgy charm.

1928 W. Division
(773) 645.3667
Division

The Smoke Daddy

"WOW!" Reads the sign above The Smoke Daddy, most likely referring to the

Ginbucks: This self-proclaimed "urban lounge" attracts a more preppy-chic crowd than most other Wicker Park bars and grills. Think a sophisticated sports bar where your metrosexual friends will have no problem lounging back with the guys and sipping Ginbuck's signature drink of the same name-a gin, ginger ale, lemon juice concoction for only $2. Touches of elegance spot the bar décor as well as the menu: look for those Cornish hens.
1469 N. Milwaukee, (773) 384.1439, Damen

magnificent whiff of barbecue when you walk through the front door. Grilling aprons along with pictures of blues and jazz artists line the aqua walls of the neighborhood joint which houses music of those genres nightly. Of course baby back ribs are the staple dish at The Smoke Daddy, but those looking for a bargain may frequent the restaurant on Thursdays when all burgers are half off.

1804 W. Division
(773) 772.6656
Division

Souk

Venture into the Middle East when you enter Souk, a classy Middle Eastern and Mediterranean restaurant. Ornate rugs and luscious paisley fabrics give an elegant flare to the restaurant's adobe walls sprinkled with candlelight. The striking atmosphere, mirrors Souk's authentic Middle Eastern dishes: servers suggest lamb, chicken or steak kabobs, or traditional starters like hummus, falafel and babba ghanoush. Be sure to stay late for the smokey and stylish atmosphere complete with apple flavored hookahs, live music and belly dancers.

409 W. Huron
(773) 227.1818
Chicago

Blu Fin

Peaking at the Polaroids that fill the entrance of Blu Fin, you'll notice pictures of Will Ferrell, Emma Thompson and Dustin Hoffman posing with the staff. It is at that moment that you'll realize Blu Fin is the most posh sushi bar in town. The graffiti walls lead you into a candle-lit lounge where the young and hip can dine on one of five specialty sushi rolls. Come Thursdays if you wanna party with the sushi chef. DJs spin and drinks are half off.

1952 W. North
(773) 394.7373
Damen

Club Lucky

This swanky Italian supper club takes patrons of Club Lucky back to the classy cocktail lounges of the 1940s. Chicagoans flock to Club Lucky for the friendly-service and huge portions of pasta dishes like homemade lasagna and homemade ravioli, as well as House and Chef Specialties like garnished chicken breast, veal and a few vegetarian plates. Stop by the '50s themed ritzy cocktail lounge lined with red naugahyde booths after your meal to sip on their famous Killer Martini, a mix of premium vodkas and gins topped with stuffed blue cheese and anchovy olives.

1824 W. Wabansia
(773) 244.0989
Damen

Bucktown & Wicker Park 73

to shop.

s, Freak Shop, Saucy Comic Books, Recycled Clothing, Life-Size She Devil, Sucked In, Po

Niche Footwear

Lacoste loafers and even some Chicago-designer shoes get plenty of leg room at this upscale shoe boutique. Most of the shoes are the designer versions of your favorite styles, but a few are definitely worth a look. Be sure to check out the great selection of Havaianas flip-flops for a fun deal. But beware: some of the sale shoes are more than $200. Probably best if you're looking to splurge-shoes can always make an outfit and this is definitely the place to look.

1566 N. Damen
(773) 489.2001
Damen

Daffodil Hill

Daffodil Hill exudes cuteness and clothes you can't find at the Gap. While prices are excessive, this Bucktown boutique is more accessible than many of the more elitist, trendy boutiques that surround it. Its cottage-style furniture and hand-made keepsakes like the paper bag scrapbook, both for sale and as décor, make it easy to forget about the store's colorful hand-knit cardigans and flowy skirts. Daffodil Hill even has a few sale racks for the price-tag conscious shopper.

1659 N. Damen
(773) 489.0101
Damen

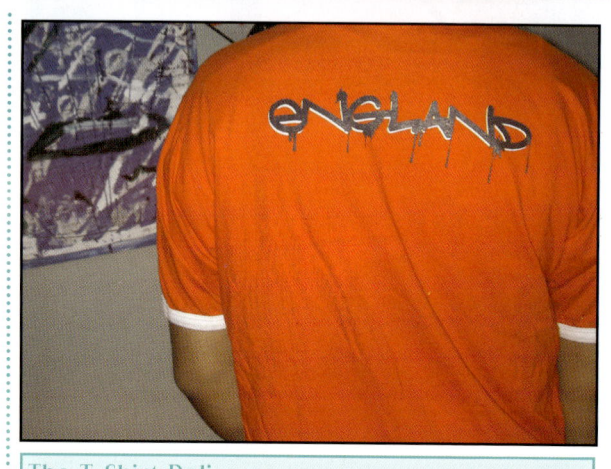

The T-Shirt Deli: If you're looking for a truly original style, start with the basics and get a slice of the T-shirt Deli. This made-to-order tee bar allows customers to take an American Apparel shirt and add some flair with decals or fuzzy letters. Options are plentiful, but a bit overpriced. But if you're itching to spread your own gospel and don't mind paying a publishing fee, make this your neighborhood deli-meat-netting, potato chips and real over-the-counter service included.
1739 N Damen, (773) 276.6266, Damen

Quimby's

Quimby's has a specific mission that would please any hipster, specializing in "the importation, distribution, and sale of unusual publications, aberrant periodicals, saucy comic booklets and assorted fancies as well as a comprehensive miscellany of the latest independent 'zines' that all the kids have been talking about." This charming and eclectic bookstore offers curious titles for all. Flip through Quimby's odd collection of irreverent books and local literary zines on the store's only couch adorned with a life-size red she-devil.

1854 W. North
(773) 342.0910
Damen

Hot Pink

Hot Pink is a refreshing stop in a neighborhood that exudes urban hipster. It is one-stop shopping for girls' night out: moderate to high-priced tops and dresses that are shiny, sexy and show skin. Besides with an outfit you'll know no one else will have, you can leave with "Takeouts: The Better Boob

Bucktown & Wicker Park

Job": $40 bra lines made from silicone that boast greater comfort than most padding. It seems Hot Pink is a very supportive shop, in more ways than one.

1464 N. Milwaukee
(773) 227.7477
Damen

Apartment Number 9

The perfect place for a truly stylish man to live, this homey boutique offers everything from cuff-links to seasonably spring pastel pink shirts. Picture a nice boutique for women, then add a little bit of rustic wood mixed in with fashionable clothing for the sexually-questionable male. With an amazing designer jean selection, this is the place to go if you're looking for a denim selection. And the best part: free beer and Jolly Ranchers are offered to the mostly affluent clientele.

1804 N. Damen
(773) 395.2999
Damen

Myopic Books

This used book store provides a microcosmic glimpse of the area's most eclectic in books, store management and customers. Bags must be checked upon entrance into the store; customers are given tags with the name of an author, as collateral. Books run the gamut from used copies of "The DaVinci Code" to seedier books in glass cases on topics such as "Indoor Marijuana Horticulture." The folks at Myopic Books also offer guests a cup of coffee for just $1.

1564 N. Milwaukee
(773) 862.4882
Damen

Recycle Men's and Women's Wear

Though Recycle features used men's and women's clothing and shoes, it strays from being tagged dingy and ultra-vintage. Recycle's décor is simple and offers bargains on used name-brand items from Gap to Gucci. It's hard to say what you'll find looking through the racks, but there definitely are some surprising and sought-after finds.

1558 N. Milwaukee
no phone
Damen

Una Mae's Freak Boutique

Finally, the proper fusion of new and used trendy apparel and accessories can be found within one store. The store seems to have gathered items not staying within a particular price or style. As a result, new Le Tigre track jackets are stacked neatly against a limited-selection $10 T-shirt rack. Amidst some of the clutter, be sure to check out the clever journals made out of vintage books (including the Holy Bible) and beautiful home wares tucked into the corners.

1422 N Milwaukee
(773) 276.7002
Damen

Untitled

The ultimate stop for the kids-who-wear-blazers club, Untitled has an amazing selection of young and hip designers. Fun T-shirts, Diesel jeans and just about every other label cover this warehouse space. Open just over a year, this is the second location for the urban mecca, who caterers to the socially-conscious by advertising for concerts and DJs at area venues. If you have a flair for the unique-but-not-too-unique, you might get sucked in. But beware: the sale rack isn't worth it.

1649 N. Damen
(773) 227.3402
Damen

Myopic Books

Bucktown & Wicker Park 75

Reckless Records: Looking for an album stop that sells more Iggy Pop than "Dirty Pop," be sure to check out the new-and-used selection at Reckless Records. Prices are moderate with the best bargains in their ironically mainstream DVD selection (a copy of the first season of "The O.C." can be found for $15 under retail). Records are varied in price and selection, but focus more on the indie crowd than any other genre. Be sure to pick up the records made into bowls, a catch at only $12.
1532 N Milwaukee, (773) 235.3727, **Damen**

Brown Elephant

If you were planning on going thrift shopping, why not help support the Howard Brown Gay Youth center by shopping at this cheaper-than-cheap thrift store. Selection is not the greatest, but prices can't be beat. T-shirts are all $3 and shoes are all $5, just to give you an example. And if you're looking for some cool furnishings and have a car to spare, the Brown Elephant offers everything from basic to antique with some definitely ugly thrown in.

3651 N. Halsted
(773) 549.5945
Addison

U S #1

Just as simple as the name comes the shopping in this mammoth thrift store. Everything is priced en masse, with walls of denim jackets selling for $35 and other items priced on a poster. If you're into rummaging, you can find a jacket or shirt or even cowboy boots for a reasonable price. And as for the those sought-after polos and jackets, don't even look at other thrift stores; just stop by here and peruse the wracks of alligator-adorned vintage wear.

1509 N. Milwaukee
(773) 489.9428
Damen

Orange Skin

If you frequent the Art Institute or Museum of Contemporary Art, the furniture and every-day houseware at Orange Skin may not seem as futuristic as it does to the casual eye. Designers from Italy, England and Spain fill the showroom with manual cameras, orange elevated dog houses and curved containers for baked goods that smell like, you guessed it, baked goods. Visit their showroom downtown if you can't get enough.

1429 N. Milwaukee
(773) 394.4500
Damen

Sound Gallery

Friends of vinyl, say hello to Sound Gallery. With a modest new and used music collection of pretty typical genres, don't come in expecting to find import treasures. Preview what you buy on open turntables while browsing the local art, music-related T-shirts and old concert posters all for sale. Though CD-less, Sound Gallery does have a fine collection of new and used turntables. Even barely usable turntables are sold.

1821 W. North
(773) 235.8472
Damen

Eurotrash

Don't think of poorly dressed European club junkies when you think of this boutique. Eurotrash, the store, at least, is an eclectic collection of trendy and chic clothing for guys and girls. Reasonably priced for the quality of clothing, racks of printed tees, unisex denim

76 Bucktown & Wicker Park

and vintage European sports jerseys attract younger clientele, as well as their Saturday martini mixer with an in-store DJ. Eurotrash also does many cross-promotions with neighborhood bars like fashion shows, VIP passes and concert ticket giveaways.

2136 W. Division
no phone
49 to Division

Shred Shop

A typical skate shop in a not-so-typical part of town. Though you don't normally see Wicker Park locals skateboarding down Division, (they opt for brightly colored retro bikes), the regular crowd from high schoolers to yuppies know where to come for skateboard repairs, snowboard tuning and the latest in skate culture. Volcom trucker hats, Reef sandals and DC shoes are among the most popular skate garb, while decks and wheels can be purchased right next to a case full of pro DVDs.

2048 W. Division
(773) 384.2100
70 to Damen

Mrs. Catwalk

This upscale boutique may have limited inventory, but the range of styles varies from the glamourous, socialite name-brand fashions from BCBG, to Urban Outfitters-like slogan T-shirts like "Trix are for Kids" and "Diet Squirt." Female friendly with pink décor and a pink spin-off of Burberry plaid for packaging, it's up to the customer to decide if the prices are worth the few items Mrs. Catwalk offers.

1810 N. Damen
no phone
73 to Damen

Raizy D'Etre

Raizy D'Etre is the pleasurable paradise for high-end lingerie and loungewear. Silk chemises and lacey garments for $200 hang luxuriously around the store while $10 multi-colored boy shorts and thongs are pinned to pink panels on the walls. Intimate and feminine, Raizy doesn't stick to selling lingerie like the popular Le Mystere bra, but also sells beauty and skincare products. On-staff makeup consultants give sample make-up applications for $58 and special services like brow-shaping are also available.

1944 N. Damen
(773) 227.2221
Damen

G Boutiques

G Boutiques is named such for a reason: the store has a generous supply of intimate wear for the boudoir and accessories. Along with sheik lingerie brands like Cosabella-the brand Britney Spears made en vogue-the store carries an array of vibrators, lubricants, sex games and toys. All accessories come with written recommendations and guides on how to use them so you don't have to feel embarrassed and ask.

2131 N. Damen
(773) 235.1234
50 to Webster

Noir

At Noir, you buy clothes to be seen in them. The boutique is even decorated like a club with funky mirrors and electric blue dressing room doors. Every-day garb is twisted into elaborate creations: collared shirts are adorned with frilled ties, cotton skirts are given multiple layers of sequence, and little black dresses' necklines plunge from heavy silver broaches. With clothes and accessories reasonably priced, girls should flock here, and guys should run down the street to the male counterpart.

1726 W. Division
(773) 489.1957
70 to Paulina

to play.

...e, Hybrid, PDA, Hip 60 Year Olds, Crossbones, Lunar Bomb, King Pale, Back Of The All...

Nick's Beer Garden

Originally located on the corner of Halsted and Armitage, Nick's Beer garden has a stylish, under lit atmosphere…that is, it's the perfect place to shoot some pool. You'll hear last call at a little before 4 a.m., making Nick's the perfect place to stop after some of the lesser bars in the area close. With good music, a great draft beer selection and hours made to please, Nick's is the place to be.

1516 N. Milwaukee
(773) 252.1155
Damen

Pint

No themes, no music. Just pub beer, pub food and sports. Pint is the perfect place to catch a game, mainly because of the six plasma screens and an extra gathering room with a big screen TV. Be sure to catch the pub's to-die-for rib special on Mondays. You can recognize Pint by the London style telephone booth out front (which operates as the directory for the neighboring apartments). No frills, just fun.

1547 N. Milwaukee
(773) 772.0990
Damen

Big Horse

Described by the staff as a "blues bar/ Mexican dive stand," the Big Horse satisfies both your need for burritos and soulful blues music. With acts gracing the stage almost every night, most playing until 2 a.m., the Big Horse excels on feeding the late night Wicker Park crowd. Although it may seem like a dive, for good food and good music accept no substitute for the Big Horse.

1558 N. Milwaukee
(773) 278.5785
Damen

Borderline Tap

This is definitely a misnomer-Borderline Tap provides one of the trendiest, European-styled bars in the area. With DJ's at least three times a week, Borderline Tap is just as famous for its dance floor as its bar. Even on slow nights, it becomes a laid back bar with good attitude and drink selection. With a dark ambiance, a worn dance floor, and great drink specials (PBR for $2), Borderline Tap is where it's at.

1958 W. North
(773) 278.5138
Damen

Floyd's Pub

"You bet your schnitzel I'm German!" reads the sign that denotes the pub's kitchen area as well as its hybrid Kraut-Irish atmosphere. With good food, a candlelit ambiance, and an interesting game room, Floyd's is a great place to hang out, play darts and drink ale. Its local feel makes Floyd's a great place to get a leisurely meal away from the bustle of North and Milwaukee.

1944 N. Oakley
(773) 276.6060
Western

The Note

Originally called the Blue Note, this live music staple is situated in one of the first Flat Iron buildings ever made. Starting out as a traditional jazz club, the Note has now expanded its horizons to alternative and hip hop. With a very eclectic band selection gracing the stage, The Note provides a great venue for local bands to get up and play. Sunday Night Reggae is a must see.

1565 N. Milwaukee
(773) 489.0011
Damen

78 Bucktown & Wicker Park

Bucktown & Wicker Park

Gallery Cabaret

A local favorite, the Gallery is an offbeat international hybrid. With gallery art hanging around you (hence the name), Gallery also offers a stage for music, poetry, and the spoken word: Liz Phair and the Smashing Pumpkins have both graced the stage of this wonderful bar. Not only does this bar truly have the "everybody knows your name" feel, it also serves the most amazing Ale-Alpha King Pale Ale. It's like going home, but your grandfather is the bartender.

2020 N. Oakley
(773) 489.5471
Western

Lottie's

Prohibition treated Lottie's well, and so did the gangsters: the basement used to be a huge gambling scene for the local mafia. That being said, this bar has a lot of history, but just because Lottie's is old, that doesn't mean she is not trendy. This cozy bar is a great place to take a date. The beer selection is incredible, especially the should-be-famous Lunar Bomb (1 shot 99 oranges in a Blue Moon, brilliant!)

1925 W. Cortland
(773) 489.0738
50 to Cortland

Nina

This is not your grandmother's knitting shop. Oh no. Young knitters and crotcheters gather in the front couches of Nina's with food and drinks to chat and catch up while they mold their stylish creations, and this social, contemporary interaction is just what Nina herself thinks knitting is all about. Find a friendly, supportive environment with upscale, high-quality materials and modern colors and patterns. If you're not a knitter, don't panic: Nina offers a range of claases from beginning to advanced.

1655 W. Division
(773) 486.8996
70 to Ashland

Can's Bar

A great concept with great execution, Can's is a premier hang out in Wicker Park. The concept is not all that hard: the bar serves cans of beer, 40 different cans of beer, that is. Imports, domestics, alien, this place has killer specials and is one of the most adaptable bars on the Northside. Servers have PDA's making the service unbelievable: it's like you imagine the drink and its there.

1640 N. Damen
(773) 227.2277
Damen

Bucktown & Wicker Park 79

Subterranean

The music scene is what dominates this eclectic bar. Famous for both its hip hop and reggae nights, Subterranean offers a not-so-wide-open dance floor. Eclectic is the word of the day, Subterranean features almost every style of music (sans country) and has either a DJ or a live act in session on an every day basis. With enough room to sit as well as room to dance to the beats, Subterranean is a great spot to get your boogie on.

2011 W. North
(773) 278.6799
Damen

Iggy's

Shaken not stirred. Iggy's is as famous for its women as it is for its martinis. Red-hot interior, stressed metal and neon lights, as well as a cheeky monkey themed "see no evil..." décor give Iggy's an edgy flare. This pulled-down-tie styled bar gives patron an equal opportunity to eat, drink and be merry. With a dance floor, roof patio, and a sit down bar, Iggy's has at least one amicable environment for everyone.

1840 W. North
(773) 227.4449
72 to Wolcott

Neo's

Though Neo's is the oldest nightclub in Chicago, it has remained in the game for good reason. With a dark '80s twist (think the Cure, not Soft Cell), this club is renowned for its fantastic dance floor. Music ranges from new wave to punk to electronic to industrial, so you'll have to move to the pace of the DJ. Positioned in the back of an alley, Neo's is a treasure much worth the trip. Black clothes and eye liner recommended.

2350 N. Clark
(773) 528.2622
22 to Fullerton

Bucktown Pub

Imagine Cheers mixed with the Drew Carrey Show, as one bartender put it, and you have the Bucktown Pub. With a long and distinguished history, this Pub has been in service since the early days of WWII. Serving several regulars, the Pub has a wonderful blue-collar atmosphere, a great selection of beer and with enough bar practice, great friends as well.

1658 W. Cortland
(773) 394.9898
9 to Cortland

The Exit

A place Syd Vicious would be proud of. The Exit offers the traditional punk atmosphere-the skull and crossbones sign and "Ramones" sign should have tipped you off. If you're feeling naughty and looking cool, wander over late at night with your pack of punks. Great drink specials are offered, $2 dollar PBR and vodka drinks on Monday. Be prepared to have a hardcore time whenever you are at The Exit.

1315 W. North
(773) 395.2700
72 to Throop

Estelle's

Estelle's is the place where the 2 a.m.-last-call-bartenders go to hang out after work. Offering a cheap and great selection of brews and hards, Estelle's also has a wonderful selection of "just bar food." With nightly specials, and a crowd that doesn't pick up until 2 a.m., Estelle's is one of the best 4 a.m. hang outs on the Northside.

2013 W. North
(773) 782.0450
Damen

Moonshine

Forget prohibition, from Moonshine's full bar to their online brewery in the works, the upscale Southwestern bar and grill offers a number of ways to enjoy the night with your friends. Open for lunch, dinner and packed weekend Funk and Soul brunch, feast on traditional Southwestern American fare like their 16 oz. rib eye and huge taco salads. Weekends start on Wednesday at this hot spot when during the summer world-renown DJs showcase their talent for Moonshine's summer dance festivities. Every other day of the week local DJs spin to a packed house of stylish hipsters.

1824 W. Division
(773) 862.8686
70 to Wood

80 Bucktown & Wicker Park

Double Door Rock

Acting as one of the newer music venues in Chicago, the Double Door in Wicker Park caters to just about everyone. With a huge variety of musical acts and a stunning number of ways to see those bands and artists, it's no wonder that the Double Door is full capacity with 473 people almost each night. The Double Door opened its proverbial doors back in the summer of 1994 and was an instant hit with Chicagoans. The spacious interior, allowing patrons to view the concert while playing pool or reclining in the intimate upstairs lounge, compares to no other venue in Chicago.

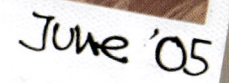

What's even more impressive is the more than friendly relationship Double Door has with the neighborhood. The venue is more than a crazy place to get into a wicked mosh pit; it acts as a musical and cultural center of the town. By playing such a wide range of music and highlighting local bands, the venue stays true to their claim of being diverse. So if you ever get an urge to play Ms. Pacman while checking out the latest and greatest bands, including Liz Phair, The Rolling Stones and Smashing Pumpkins to name a few, Double Door is the place for you.

JUNE '05

bucktown wicker park.

1572 N Milwaukee   (773) 489.3160   **Damen**

Bucktown & Wicker Park 81

Oldtown

to eat.....................Adobo Grill
                       The Fudge Pot
                 Uncle Julio's Hacienda

   to shop....................The Spice House
                              Vagabonds
                        Oldtown Gardens

   to play...................Zentra
                        Hogs n Honeys
                     Second City

82 Chicago Unzipped

Unzipped

History 101...

You'll know you're in Old Town by the almost immediate halt to gleaming money trap stores and the smaller rise of old architecture. Old Town really is as old as the Great Chicago Fire. Some surviving houses still remain, as well as a few feet of wood-paved roads that facilitated the disaster. Old Town is home to the country's oldest summer art fair, not a shocking concept as you stroll down cobblestone streets. Its visible history (and site of the Chicago Historical Society) doesn't mean Old Town's social scene is history. Treat your visiting parents to architecture tours and put them up in a respected bed and breakfast while you go out on the town. Rest up on a bench in the beautiful Washington Square Park in order to save your energy for the bars and world famous comedy club to the north. In addition to restaurants famous for tequila, the aptly named Weed Street houses theme bars that will knock your socks off.

oldtown

www.ChicagoUnzipped.com

to eat.

Five-Course, Boisterous, Cocotazo, Label Whore Cocktail, Spoon Tang, Kick Back, Prim

Cafe Sushi

White washed walls illuminated by blue lights gives this BYOB sushi restaurant a surprisingly fresh atmosphere fitting for their fast and fresh food. While Cafe Sushi's regular crowds primarily pack in on Friday and Saturday nights, weekday business is mostly limited to delivery. The young crowd enjoys the classic rock music but the early 10 p.m. closing makes this restaurant a first stop rather than a final weekend destination. During the summer, outdoor seating is a prime spot for people watching.

1342 N. Wells
(312) 337.0700
Clark/Division

LaFette

French for "The Feast," this multi-course American Bistro serves a five-course meal which includes appetizer, soup, salad, entrée and dessert. Unique combinations like the brownie banana fruit loop sundae and crab ravioli in asparagus cream sauce complement more traditional dishes like New York strip steak and porc à l'orange. A four-course brunch is also available on weekends. And consider your hangover nursed: one alcoholic beverage is included in the fixed price.

163 W. North
(312) 397.6300
Clark/Division

Adobo Grill

This upscale Mexican eatery has all the right ingredients: a boisterous, friendly atmosphere; tasty traditional dishes; and most importantly, amazing drinks. Hardcore liquor lovers can choose from 90 sipping tequilas, while mixed drinks range from the traditional house margarita, shaken tableside, to the Cocotazo, coconut sorbet and rum served in a whole coconut. Try the house specialty, Guacamole con Totopos, and save room for dessert. Be warned: these dishes are almost too pretty to eat.

1610 N. Wells
(312) 266.7999
Clark/Division

Spoon

It's easiest to describe Spoon by first saying what it's not: a dance club, a snooty VIP lounge, or a pick-up joint. Instead, this "Casual Funk and Food Joint" is a great place to sit with a group of friends, have a few cocktails-the Spoon Tang is particularly memorable-and take in some music. Appetizers, sandwiches and entrees are also available until 1 a.m. Be aware of Friday and Saturday nights: lines can surpass the hour mark.

1240 N. Wells
(312) 642.5522
Clark/Division

84 Old Town

Old Town

Close to Home, Unadorned, Personalized, Wells

Fresh Choice

Try everything and something new at a place where you can add spinach, parsley, garlic, or ginger to any fresh squeezed juice your heart desires. Boasting the "Best Smoothies in Chicago," according to CBS News, Fresh Choice gives the option of various dairy, fruit, chocolate and combined blended flavors. This place also offers various soups, salads and sandwiches that can quench any degree of hunger. Don't forget to note the 91 cents hard-boiled egg option, clearly, what every health food place is always missing.

1534 N. Wells
(312) 664.7065
Clark/Division

Stanley's Kitchen and Tap

From the rocking chairs on the front porch to the trophies and kids' drawings adorning the walls, this country-style kitchen feels as close to home as your living room couch. Nights and weekdays feature a menu of classic comfort foods: mac and cheese, mashed potatoes and fried chicken are a few favorites, while weekends bring an all-you-can-eat breakfast buffet. A true family restaurant, Stanley's is a great place to bring your kids-or at least those brats you baby-sit.

1970 N. Lincoln
(312) 642.0007
Fullerton

Adobo Grill

The Fudge Pot

Functioning as a drive-thru catering to chocolate cravings, customers walk through a small hallway, unadorned besides overwhelming chocolate aroma, to place their orders. Requests consist of the standard truffles and fudge, but personalized items can also be created. Whether to satisfy a chocolate binge or commission 100 chocolate fur coats for a friend's "Welcome to the Windy City" party, the Fudge Pot will more than satisfy your sweet tooth.

1532 N. Wells
(312) 943.1777
Clark/Division

Old Town 85

to shop.

e T-shirt, First Class, Secret Pleasures, Taste of the World, Dangly, Walled Rainbow, Lic

Sara Jane

This chic boutique's collection ranges from subtle embellishments to the classic white T-shirt to sleek formal wear and business attire. Have a question about an item? The manager will be happy to help, and will even speed dial the designer for assistance. Stylish buys and first class treatment do come at a price more suited for those already receiving a real paycheck rather than those still interviewing.

49 E. Oak
(312) 751.0669
Clark/Division

The Spice House

It's an unspoken rule that the secret to a dish is not the actual food, but the flavor. With a sample of every seasoning, Spice House offers a five course meal in powdered form. From Taco Nacho flavoring to traditional Adobo herbs, enjoy a taste of the world one glass container at a time. You can clear your palate with a cup of water on the house. While you might be overwhelmed by the mosaic of aromas when you walk in, the prices aren't nearly as shocking.

1512 N. Wells
(312) 274.0378
Clark/Division

String a Strand on Wells

Not only is it cheaper to make your own jewelry, but you can make it the perfect shade or length. Take a stroll and see beads from around the world on display, and if you have the time, take a seat and get creative. Whether it's earrings, a necklace, or anklet, this place provides the materials for a unique dangly accessory. While the walled rainbow of natural stones can get expensive, search the table tops for unique treasures in the more affordable range.

1444 N. Wells
(312) 335.1930
Clark/Division

Old Town Aquarium

Escape the cold and windy streets with this tropical heaven. Besides the numerous aquariums and accessories on sale, walk the aisles and gawk at tanked tropical wonders. From blowfish and lion fish, or your own little Nemo, there are numerous colorful friends you can take home. Before you get too excited, it's important to remember that bringing a sample of tank water is the only way these protective owners will part with the shop's rarities.

1538 N. Wells
(312) 642.8763
Clark/Division

86 Old Town

inding Nemo, # Old Town Brighten Up, Big Boys, Black Tru

Old Town Gardens

Nothing compares to the scent and colors of an open air, fresh flower market in the middle of a Chicago street. Come spring and summer, venture over and pick up beautiful flowers to brighten up your home or maybe even someone's day. From pots and hangers to bushes and trees, these plants come in all shapes and sizes. While the prices are fairly reasonable, the effect of the flowers is damn near priceless.

1555 N. Wells
(312) 266.6300
Clark/Division

Up Down Tobacco

We're not talking about some head-shop where dreaded teenagers drool over blown glass; this place is where the big boys hang out. With cigars from every corner of the world and prices ranging from $1 to a whopping $40 a cigar, you can find that perfect manly gift. This is the place for that perfect Hitchcock pipe, and a wall full of tobacco for sale by weight boasts flavors like Black Truffle Crème Brule and Mom's Norwegian Shag.

1550 N. Wells
(312) 337.8505
Clark/Division

Old Town 87

to play.

Longest Ride, Prestigious, Improvised, Jock-Friendly, Buzz, Beer-Guzzling, Tequila Club

Roadhouse

Loved by beer-guzzling college students, hardcore shot junkies and bar-top dancing divas alike, the Roadhouse takes its honky-tonk status seriously. A bar-side saddle, complete with a sink-like basin, allows bartenders to pour shots directly into bar-goers' waiting mouths, while bench-style car seats and old gas pumps line the walls. As an added incentive, "Tequila Club Card" holders are given a free T-shirt after taking their 25th shot. Alcohol poisoning is sold separately.

1653 N. Wells
(312) 440.0535
North/Clybourn

The Second City

The prestigious claim to alumni such as Chris Farley is understated by Second City's comfortable and casual environment. "Just a comedy club" falls terribly short of the level of intellectual and political satire mixed into improvised and rehearsed skits. With first come, first serve seating, arriving an hour early and enjoying a cocktail and dessert before the show will help you avoid having the back wall for a head rest.

1616 N. Wells
(312) 337.3992
Clark/Division

North Beach Chicago

At this bar, the beer is served with a side of sweat. In a semi-bizarre combination, North Beach is a jock-friendly gym-slash-bar where you can get your workout on the sand volleyball courts while getting a nice little buzz during your "water" breaks. For those who'd rather stay sweat-free, there are also pool tables, darts, arcade games and a few bowling lanes. The dress is casual, as is the atmosphere, so leave your stilettos at home. As for jockstraps, it's your call.

1551 N. Sheffield
(312) 266.7842
North/Clybourn

Hogs and Honeys: A mechanical bull challenges customers to put down their beer and compete with their friends for the longest ride. Cheering mixes with the pop rock, not country, songs playing overhead, adding to the already wild atmosphere with the chaotic license-plate-covered-walls. Located in the Weed Street District, Hogs and Honeys' fun-loving personality sets it apart from the other bars nearby, making it a not-to-be missed experience. **871 N. Sheffield** (312) 397.1277 **North/Clybourn**

Old Town

Joe's Sports Bar

This massive establishment is all about sports, sports fans, beer, and of course, beer fans. Jerseys and baseball hats dominate the daytime crowd's attire-most of whom are there to watch one of the seemingly hundreds of TVs while the late-night crowd brings a more casually trendy feel. Wednesdays and Saturday nights bring live music, adding yet another element to this multi-purpose sports bar/nightclub/music venue. Bring a few bucks and your game face; just leave the body paint at home.

940 W. Weed
(312) 337.3486
North/Clybourn

Burton Place

This "sports café" has all the elements of the classic neighborhood pub: beer, burgers, darts, billiards, friendly bartenders, and of course, loyal regulars. Extra-late weeknight hours-the bar is open until 4 a.m. Monday through Friday-are a plus, and post-gig visits from Second City comedians keep the crowd interesting. Remember this place.

1447 N. Wells
(312) 664.4699
Clark/Division

Twin Anchors

Remember that quaint little restaurant from "Return To Me"-that slightly twisted romantic comedy about the guy who falls in love with the recipient of his dead wife's heart transplant? The real version of that restaurant is none other than Twin Anchors Restaurant and Tavern, a 73-year-old Chicago institution. When it's not serving as a movie set however, Twin Anchors serves up burgers, steaks and seafood at pleasantly low prices. Get there early, lines are long, and order the ribs.

1655 N. Sedgwick
(312) 266.1616
North/Clybourn

Zentra

This Hindi-themed dance club offers a different attitude five nights each week: Three Degrees Ultra Lounge Mondays, Ill Noise Thursdays, Sweet & Lowdown Fridays, Dirty Saturdays, and gay-focused On The Down Low Sundays. Each night differs in dress code, cover charge, and music genre (the general trend is towards house and hip-hop). Save a few bucks at the door by putting yourself on the guest list-the feelings of self-importance and VIP status are worth the hassle.

923 W. Weed
(312) 642.5522
North/Clybourn

Ethnic Chicago

Residents know that Chicago feels like the smallest big city in the world. Find out why by trekking Chicago's ethnic neighborhoods

Greektown

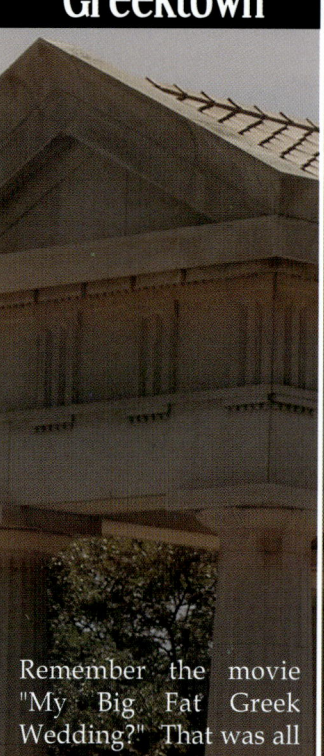

Remember the movie "My Big Fat Greek Wedding?" That was all real. Greektown, complete with a monument of a Greek temple, is exactly what you think it would be. The streets are lined with flashy cars and the late-night crowd is pretty ritzy.

UIC-Halsted

Little Italy

Want real Italian Ice? Head over to Mario's in Little Italy and see why there's always a crowd outside the stand. In the midst of being completely renovated, Little Italy is an up-and-coming area filled with incredible tributes to the bigger Italy. Make sure to stop by the sports museum while you're there.

Polk

Chinatown

Once you step into the Chinatown, it's easy to forget that you can still see the skyline. Filled with cute and cheap boutiques and even cheaper restaurants, Chinatown is worth an entire day's visit. The streets are always busy, making this a lively neighborhood.

Cermak/Chinatown

Chicago Unzipped

Unzipped

You can't unzip Chicago until you've set foot in these places:

Bridgeport

end enough time here you might see Chicago ayor Richard M. Daley und Polo Café. Home the Chicago White Sox, dgeport is a popular th-side stop. Check out bars and restaurants in area, many of which r to the baseball ionados.

Sox-35th

Bronzeville

Bronzeville has been called one of the nation's most prominent sites of African-American urbanization in the early 20th century. The streets are lined with numerous statues in tribute to that time period. The area is also known as the blues district.

35-Bronzeville-IIT

Pilsen

The best word to describe Pilsen is authentic. Be ready for a rough and tough feel to this area and some sometimes-dodgy restaurants. The best food is from the street-vendors but the area is steeped in an enormous amount of history and culture.

Hoyne

www.ChicagoUnzipped.com 91

River North

to eat.................Frontera Grill
                      Melting Pot
                      F212
to shop...............The Lego Store
                      Marshall Fields
                      Smoke Shop
to play...............10 Pin Bowling Lounge
                      Rockit Bar and Grill
                      City Pool Hall

Unzipped

A hidden treasure...

Known among artsy yuppies for its numerous art galleries, River North surprises the Chicago novice with its late night scene and exciting restaurants.

Switching from predictable chains to offbeat local color from one block to the next makes the neighborhood palatable for all tastes. If you've stayed out past 2 a.m. in the city, chances are you wandered into River North, whose war time industry nickname of "Smokey Hollow" can now apply to its darkly entertaining late night clubs. You'll wonder with each opening how another bar will fit onto Hubbard Street or how another gallery can survive in the west, but you'll certainly check them both out. River North is home to some of the most fun and funky restaurants that make the few westward blocks from Chicago's main drag more than worth the while. With the river blocking the seriousness of the financial Loop to the south, and the Gold Coast skyline to the east providing the view, River North feels like a secret enclave within Chicago that the everyday tourist doesn't catch on a tour.

www.ChicagoUnzipped.com

to eat.

...d Network, Greesy Cheese Fries, Mock-Rudeness, Star-Studded, Glowing Orbs, Roofto...

Mambo Grill

Boasting an extensive rum and tequila selection, Mambo Grill's cocina Latina mixes a south of the border fiesta with tasty South American cuisine. The space is equally divided between the bar and dining space, keeping a perfect balance between fine dining and celebrating. Daily drink specials on margaritas, mojitos and sangria complement dinner, and the bar just steps away keeps the party going.

412 Clark
(312) 467.9797
Grand

Ed Debevic's

A Chicagoland favorite, Ed Debevic's is a '50s style diner with an attitude. Oldies blast overhead, kids run between arcade games, and customers laugh at the mock-rudeness that defines the service. This diner is a unique and lively spot to chow down on traditional diner favorites like burgers, chili, cheese fries and shakes. Like all popular restaurant landmarks, you can purchase every type of memorabilia imaginable after your unforgettable experience there.

640 N. Wells
(312) 664.1707
Chicago

Blue Water Grill

Leave your lobster bib at home when you dine at this new-to-Chicago seafood restaurant. Chic and spacious, Blue Water Grill has a "see and be seen" feel, especially in the downstairs sushi bar and lounge where you can mingle with friends or flirt with the attractive staff. If you can't decide on an entrée, splurge on the chilled shellfish castle, a tower of seven different types of shellfish topped off with a one-pound lobster.

520 N. Dearborn
(312) 777.1400
Grand

Frontera Grill/Topolobambo

Getting a kick out of dining at a celebrity chef's restaurant will cost a pretty penny at either of these two adjoining restaurants. While Frontera Grill is designed to be a scaled down version of Topolobambo, entrees still range in the $20s. Beyond the fame factor, the food is worth the cost, but you'll need to know more Spanish than "taco" or "burrito" to understand the menu. Scope out the Saturday brunch for a less crowded and more accessible experience.

445 N. Clark
(312) 661.1434
Grand

Chilpancingo

One local vented, "No, it's not a good Mexican restaurant, there's no chips and salsa on the table and you can't just get a taco." A Mexican Chef's Association Award would disagree with her assessment, but be warned Chilpancingo is a far cry from Taco Bell. The smell of fresh tortillas overwhelms as you enter a space filled with paper magnolias overhead. While the food is gourmet, the prices are relatively low, a bonus of having an ex-Topolobambo chef in the kitchen.

358 W. Ontario
(312) 266.9525
Chicago

Harry Caray's

With approximately 1500 baseball memorabilia items, Harry Caray's steakhouse is practically a museum of baseball legends. The national praise showered on this Italian steakhouse over

94 River North

River North

the decades is received with warm Midwestern friendliness just as one would expect from a restaurant named after the late Hall of Fame baseball announcer Harry Caray. Make reservations or just drop in to enjoy the relaxed environment and the mouth-watering cuisine.

33 W. Kinzie
(312) 828.0966
Grand

Sushi Samba

The spacious sushi bar and cocktail lounge provides visual stimulation that rivals how the sushi creations tantalize taste buds. With mosaic backdrops, draped beaded ceiling fixtures and orange and green curved walls, it's no wonder this high cost, high quality sushi extravaganza attracts such a chic, young, celebrity-studded crowd.

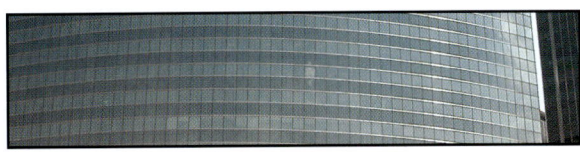

The roof top lounge has a ritzy pool house feel and is filled with plush, colorful couches that invite indulgences from the full dinner and drink menu.

504 N. Wells
(312) 595.2300
Merchandise Mart

Brett's Kitchen

Nestled among River North's maze of art galleries, there is a quaint lunch spot right under the el. Eye the pastries in cases, fresh fruit on display, or the sandwiches listed on chalkboards, but spy the professional black and white photograph of the staff to remember you're in the art district. If the galleries are too intimidating, cozy up in Brett's Kitchen for food to revitalize. Perhaps Brett's breakfast will give you the fortitude to properly gallery-hop.

233 W. Superior
(312) 664.6354
Chicago

Osteria Via Stato

At the 75-seat wine bar, customers enjoy the extensive wine selection by the glass, quartino, or through the tasting program, in which a trio of choices are served at three different price levels. Dinner and lunch begin with a generous serving of antipasti, followed by different smaller portions, and if it's possible to still eat more, mouth-watering house gelati. The service, like the food and wine, live up to their culturally rich and amiable Italian reputation.

620 N. State
(312) 642.8450
Grand

Tizi Melloul

The red mosaic entry way winds you around from a street in Chicago to a restaurant in the Mediterranean, maybe all the way to Mt. Tizi Melloul in Morocco. This restaurant and lounge offers three ways to enjoy your dining experience: in the spirit of Mediterranean style you can eat with your hands in the Crescent room; more formally in the Main Dining Room; or more casually in the posh, all-white lounge.

531 N. Wells
(312) 670.4338
Merchandise Mart

Al's Italian Beef

If you are curious what an Italian Beef Sandwich is, take a peek at the hunk of shredded beef leaking torrents of juice down a diner's chin. Sinatra-like Italian music lures customers in from the street, but the music ceases indoors where the fight between man and sandwich begins. Be safe and order a hotdog with great fries, but the Italian beef is what true Chicagoans cater parties with.

169 W. Ontario
(312) 943.3222
Chicago

Vong's Thai Kitchen

What started as an upscale, New York-based restaurant has since expanded to Chicago, offering the same legendary taste with a much more reasonable price tag. The restaurant's atmosphere is laid-back but still ritzy enough to impress a date (order her the Thai-jito and she will be yours). For dinner you can't go wrong with the Pad Thai or curry dishes.

6 W. Hubbard
(312) 644.8664
Grand

Bin 36

Nothing kills a restaurant experience like the intimidation of a snobby waiter and a cryptic wine menu. Learn the ropes at Bin 36, a restaurant, tavern and wine store that aims to take the pain out of wine education. Guests can sample 50 different wines while the staff gives tips on how to choose wines that best complement their meal choices. Afterwards, they can purchase their favorites at retail prices.

339 N. Dearborn
(312) 755.9463
Grand

Alibi

A "2 slices for $5" lunch special identifies the two strengths and weaknesses of the pizza parlor. The slices aren't that big, and the main appeal is eating pizza at 4 a.m. on weekends. The perfect location on bar-packed Hubbard St. ensures a lively crowd at all hours, where perhaps patrons are too drunk to care about slice size but can obey their late

The Melting Pot

In a word, cheesy is the overriding theme at this corporate chain restaurant. Though the atmosphere is lacking-the Melting Pot shares an entrance with a tanning salon, giving the air a distinct potency of coconut oil and melted cheese-it can be forgiven through its mouth-watering four-course selections of fondue. If you are not up for drenching your tenderloin in white wine and garlic swiss, make sure to indulge in a decadent chocolate fondue dessert. **609 N. Dearborn** (312) 573.0011 **Chicago**

night craving without going home and waiting for delivery.

23 W. Hubbard
(312) 464.0609
Grand

Mr. Beef

A sign on the outside says, "Enjoy our elegant dinning room." That is a lie. There are no stools, everyone stands crowded, and the sandwiches are worth it. What is true about Mr. Beef, however, is its cult-like popularity. You'll actually recognize faces from the celebrity wall (albeit in headshots from the '80s) and encounter a line in the middle of the afternoon for one of their Italian beef sandwiches.

666 N. Orleans
(312) 337.8500
Chicago

Fogo de Chao

When standard dorm chicken makes you want to cry, head over to the "churrascaria" (Brazilian for ridiculous amounts of meat) to gorge. Slabs of various meats roast in the street facing window, only a hint of what costumed waiters bring to the table continuously until you flip a card to stoplight red. Drag a vegetarian past the red meat spectacle and sate them with the mile long salad bar with asparagus like baseball bats.

661 N. LaSalle
(312) 932.9330
Chicago

L8

On a street too cool for real names, L8 incorporates a number. Other bar-lined streets have late night diners or pizza, but W. Ontario St. has late night gourmet. After sinking a whole pay-check into the bottle services at neighboring establishments, the wood-fired pizzas and specialty pastas won't seem that expensive. Where else can you sate your late night carpaccio and tiramisu craving?

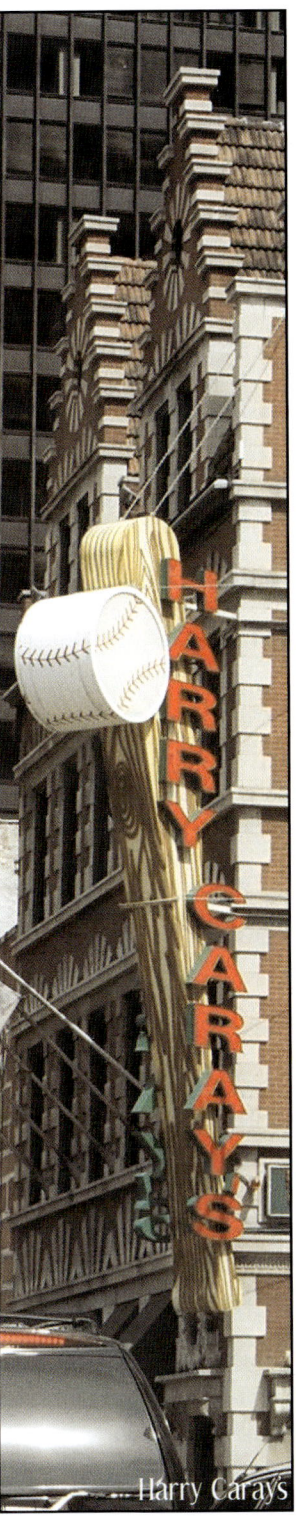

222 W. Ontario
(312) 266.0616
Chicago

Brasserie Jo

Ever wish people still wore classy hats like in the forties? Brasserie Jo thinks so enough to have "Les Chapeaux of Brasserie Jo" Thursdays where wearing a hat will garner a free dessert. While this French restaurant is still an upscale restaurant by all means, being the baby of famous Chef Jean Joho means you're getting a bargain by way of good cuisine. Daily specials include frog legs to test your commitment to the French dining experience.

59 W. Hubbard
(312) 595.0800
Grand

Karyn's Cooked

You don't have to be a vegan to crave one of Karyn's mouth-watering completely animal free dishes. The yellow, orange and bamboo décor creates a soothing retreat from the busy city. Karyn's "conscious comfort food" is a nutritional way to decompress and indulge that's not at the expense of a furry friend. Both the prices and the plates are pleasantly light.

738 N. Wells
(312) 587.1050
Chicago

Nacional 27

Pairing salsa with salsa dancing, Nacional 27 covers all the bases of the 27 Latin countries whose food it represents. Each night has its own special, including a wine night that donates to the homeless, to lure you in before the busy weekends. Try the ceviche sampler to learn what it is (raw fish in a citrus marinade) and that you love it. Learning doesn't stop there with a menu so full of regional specialties you'll want your pocket dictionary.

325 W. Huron
(312) 664.2727
Chicago

Cyrano's Bistrot, Wine Bar and Cabaret

Being both a restaurant and a cabaret allows Cyrano's Bistrot to fully conjure south western France with food, images, and song. Specials like a four course meal and admission to a slide show or jazz singer distinguish Cyrano's from other bistros that have dropped the French "t." Adding to authenticity, only French wine is served, selected by the chef's wife while abroad. The colorful décor and menu items like a pâté sampler make the bistrot a warm welcome to French cuisine.

546 N. Wells
(312) 467.0546
Grand

F212

When the neighborhood coffee shop isn't trendy enough, head to F212 where honey is served in test tubes and pixie sticks sit on tables where sugar should be. A wide variety of tea and coffee is complemented by mini cakes and tarts almost too picturesque to eat and a whole freezer of gelato by the pint. The neon walls and a molecular sculpture of caffeine overhead remind you that F212 is really, really cool.

401 N. Wells
(312) 670.4212
Merchandise Mart

Iguana Café

This little eclectic café, nearly hidden by its remote location, features a restaurant and coffee shop in one. Catch a quick caffeine jolt accompanied by a delicious European style pastry or sandwich, or chow down on their ever-so-popular crepes with a glass of wine. Whether you go for sweet or salty, these delicious French treats hit the spot every time. Enjoy your dining experience with the café's iguana mascot looking at you from its glass tank.

517 N. Halsted
(312) 432.0563
Grand

98 River North

to shop.

Funky, Emasculate, Late Night Soiree, Toys, **River North**, Unzip.

Equinox

Although from the street this shop looks like your mother's antique store, a walk inside reveals a wide selection of funky purses and jewelry alongside unique furniture, light fixtures and picture frames. Equinox is the perfect place to find a birthday gift for your roommate or an apartment-warming present for yourself. The prices are reasonable and it's worth a walk-through to see what tickles your fancy, be it a couch or a necklace.

609 N. State
(312) 335.8006
Grand

Doolin's

Whether you're interested in a fog machine for your late-night soirée, or a bubble machine for a niece's birthday party, Doolin's endless supplies are available at their store or by delivery. Every party needs some toys, and with this three-generation-old party supply store there's no excuse too small for a celebration. So, go ahead: if you've made it to another Friday, put up banners, blow up balloons, and start the festivities!

511 N. Halsted
(312) 243.9424
Grand

American Male

Metrosexuals go to salons; real men come to American Male for a "barbering experience." While offering services such as paraffin dips along with hair cuts and shaves, American Male is careful not to emasculate by immediately offering a complementary beer and relying on clever wording (a manicure here is actually a hand detailing service). With leather couches, jerseys on walls, and games played on three TVs, men almost forget where they are . . . and that's the point.

401 W. Ontario
(312) 482.8170
Belmont

River North 99

Rock 'n Roll Mickey D's Style

river north

100 River North

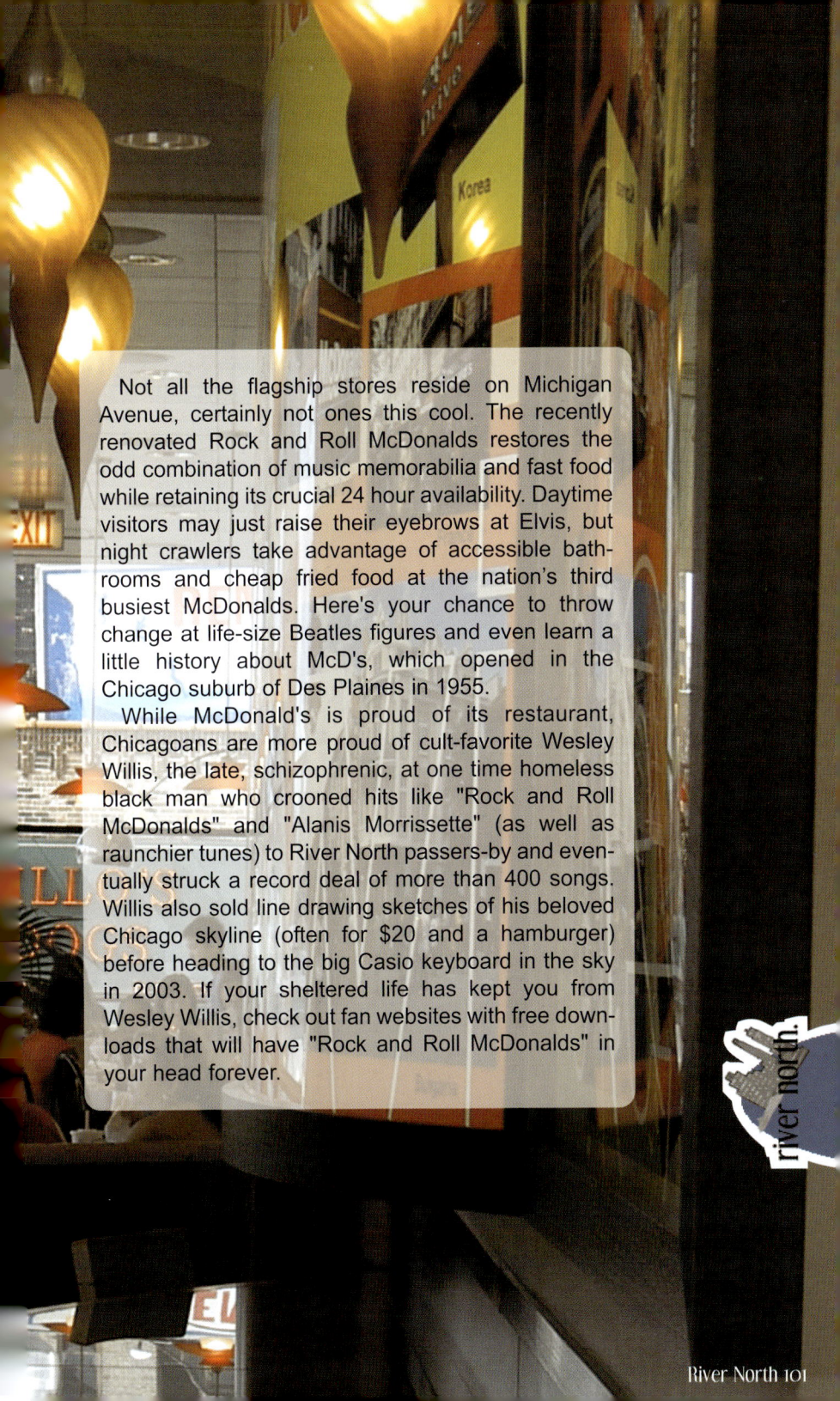

Not all the flagship stores reside on Michigan Avenue, certainly not ones this cool. The recently renovated Rock and Roll McDonalds restores the odd combination of music memorabilia and fast food while retaining its crucial 24 hour availability. Daytime visitors may just raise their eyebrows at Elvis, but night crawlers take advantage of accessible bathrooms and cheap fried food at the nation's third busiest McDonalds. Here's your chance to throw change at life-size Beatles figures and even learn a little history about McD's, which opened in the Chicago suburb of Des Plaines in 1955.

While McDonald's is proud of its restaurant, Chicagoans are more proud of cult-favorite Wesley Willis, the late, schizophrenic, at one time homeless black man who crooned hits like "Rock and Roll McDonalds" and "Alanis Morrissette" (as well as raunchier tunes) to River North passers-by and eventually struck a record deal of more than 400 songs. Willis also sold line drawing sketches of his beloved Chicago skyline (often for $20 and a hamburger) before heading to the big Casio keyboard in the sky in 2003. If your sheltered life has kept you from Wesley Willis, check out fan websites with free downloads that will have "Rock and Roll McDonalds" in your head forever.

river north.

to play.

to try something else.

ESPN Zone

If man's two biggest vices are sex and sports, then the two places every man needs to go before he dies are the Playboy Mansion and ESPN Zone. This 35,000-square-foot playground is an orgy of big-screen TVs, athletic iconography, cyber sports and testosterone. Highlights include the Screening Room, a 16-foot screen surrounded by skybox viewing suites, the Sports Arena arcade and the Studio Grill, which serves jock-pleasing grub like steak and chops.

43 E. Ohio
(312) 644.3776
Grand

Puerto Vallarta

Spicing things up in more ways than one, Puerto Vallarta invites customers to work up an appetite with free salsa lessons on Mondays from 6-8 p.m. Following the lesson, the dance floor is open to any more aspiring dancers for the rest of the night. Meanwhile, non-dancers crowd the bar to watch their favorite sports event, enjoy the delicious Mexican grill cooking, or drink up the courage to step in for the next song.

431 N. Wells
(312) 755.1244
Merchandise Mart

10 Pin Bowling Lounge

Chicago's downtown scene just wouldn't be complete without an upscale bowling alley to impress even non-bowlers. The nightclub quality audio system and extensive martini selection make this high-energy bowling lounge a big hit for people looking for a more exciting and hip way to enjoy appetizers and a drink or two. 10 Pin even replaces the traditional retro bowling shoes with stylish alternative options. While alcohol may not improve your game, you'll celebrate a strike that much more.

330 N. State
(312) 644.0500
Grand

City Pool Hall

This pool hall is a great place to sharpen billiard skills at any player level. A local favorite, several regulars were selected to play in the Hollywood flick "Pool Hall Junkies." Enjoy various beer specials around $2 nearly every night of the week and take it a little further on Absolut Fridays where all Absolut drinks are only $4. You can minimize your spending and maximize your drinking on Saturdays from 7a.m to 7p.m. when tables are free with just a $10 spending minimum.

640 W. Hubbard
(312) 491.9690
Grand

to bar hop.

Howl at the Moon

It's hard not to have fun belting out "Sweet Home Alabama" with a room full of drunken strangers, and Howl at the Moon offers just that. Dueling pianists lead bar-goers in a group sing-along at this rowdy, saloon-style piano bar. The staff also joins in the show, performing routines on the bar and sometimes even singing on stage. Definitely a worthy alternative to your typical bar scene.

26 W. Hubbard
(312) 863.7427
Grand

Boss Bar

The bar's name was the title of a biography of the first Mayor Daley, a jab that acknowledged not only his supreme position in Chicago politics, but also the tinge of corruption that has become a Chicago trademark. It is fitting to have Daley's face and the Chicago skyline being the only sparse decorations in this efficient bar. Few tables line the walls but the main attraction is the central, four-sided bar that serves alcohol with an ease that is the Chicago way.

420 N. Clark
(312) 527.1203
Grand

River North

...re, Guzzle Alcohol, Swank, ... *Ballar, Down, Saloon-Style*

Reserve

The fine attire required at this ultra-high end lounge seems like everyday clothing for the big spenders inside. The elite clientele are known to drop thousands for bottles of champagne, while others simply sip on an exotic martini in the crimson tinted room. Atmosphere aside, the real allure is patrons who expect nothing but the best and, hence, continually return to the Reserve. Call ahead to get on the guest list and ensure a smooth entrance.

858 W. Lake
(312) 455.1111
Clinton

Coyote Ugly Saloon

You don't need to see the movie to get the appeal of scantily clad bartenders dancing on bars and singing along to songs with coordinated dances. Antics don't stop there as tequila shots can be served spit from a bartender into a patron's bewildered mouth. Bras hang from ceiling fixtures and there is a cage in the back. Be warned: dance on the bar at your own risk as concussions are handed a free bag of ice and an aspirin.

316 W. Erie
(312) 642.2400
Chicago

Blue Frog Bar and Grill

Remember that game called Operation, where you dissect a cardboard man with a light-up nose? Go ahead and get nostalgic, because at the Blue Frog, you can enjoy your favorite board games of yesteryear along with cheap beer. This laid-back bar is the perfect atmosphere to strike up a conversation with a stranger as you try and sink their battleship-just don't be a sore loser.

676 N. Lasalle
(312) 943.8900
Grand

Rockit Bar & Grill

From the minds behind Le Passage comes a surprisingly simple bar and restaurant. In a land of clubs competing to up-swank and out-sleek each other,

Rockit Bar & Grill

Rockit's décor is minimal beyond the antler type light fixture chandeliers. The restaurant and upstairs pool tables ensure a crowd that wants more than a place to guzzle alcohol. Arrive early to avoid lines, rejoice in the lack of a cover charge, and be prepared for expensive drinks.

22 W. Hubbard
(312) 645.6000
Grand

Green Door Tavern

One of many kitschy signs says, "You are about to enter another era, enjoy it now." It is this sass that makes the Green Door Tavern everything "retro" restaurants wish they could be, especially since it dates back to the Chicago Fire. Above all the hubbub of food and drinks

River North 103

along the bar is a mounted jack rabbit head, a sanguine reminder to enjoy and not think too hard about the knick knacks.

678 N. Orleans
(312) 664.5496
Chicago

O'Leary's Public House

The story about Mrs. O'Leary's cow starting the Chicago Fire was actually an attempt to rile anti-Irish sentiment, but time and urban legends have turned the O'Leary name into one worthy of a bar and restaurant. Guinness art posters overlook the bar in a mix of Big Brother and subliminal advertising, but many non-Irish beers are also on draft. Standard bar food turns to comfort food as the bartenders strive to make everyone feel like a regular.

541 N. Wells
(312) 661.1306
Merchandise Mart

to club.

House of Blues

Featuring all types of artists, from country to rap, the House of Blues attracts the most famous musicians for consistently sold-out shows. The venue's layout provides a great view for all concert-goers, but for an even closer view of a live performance, luxurious opera boxes and the Foundation Room are available for reservations. Although overshadowed by the spectacular performances, the House of Blues also offers a full menu in their dining rooms, serving New Orleans style cooking for lunch and dinner.

329 N. Dearborn
(312) 527.2583
Clark/Lake

Funky Buddha Lounge

The unusual Indian décor only adds to the unique ethnic vibe of this bar and club. Standing out from the competition with a variety of special organic drink blends, this place offers a chill alternative to the downtown clubbing scene. Whether you lounge among the pillow adorned couches of the VIP areas or go wild on the dance floor, local DJs and musicians featured nightly pump out great beats that get your body moving.

728 W. Grand
(312) 666.1695
Grand

Exit

Spike belts, mohawks, pleather and metal are the essentials that make up this club's hardcore energy. Popular among the punk scene, this place provides a great change in atmosphere until 4 a.m. Whether you prefer to dance in cages upstairs or lounge around on the vintage motorcycles scattered on the first floor, there is no question that the crowd

Sugar: A Dessert Bar: This off-beat bar marries drinking with dessert, creating a somewhat bizarre nightclub candy shop with a twist. Designed by local celebrity Suhail (designer of the loft from MTV's Real World Chicago) the décor is a spectacle in itself, inspired by Willy Wonka's factory and complete with hard-candy stools and candy-colored walls. Menu offerings include more than two dozen desserts (though most of the hipster guests are there to do anything but eat), dessert liqueurs, cognacs, grappas and an impressive wine selection. **108 W. Kinzie** (312) 822.9999 **Merchandise Mart**

certainly knows how to have a good time. Enjoy some old school punk, ska and metal spun by local disc jockeys with nightly drink.

1315 W. North
(773) 395.2700
Bus: 72 to Throop

Sound-Bar

This bi-level, mega dance club boasts a chic décor and nine different bars, each with its own color scheme (drinks included) and ambiance. Dance floor divas will appreciate the dual dance floors where international DJs spin until 4 a.m., while the less energetic can enjoy wine and champagne in the downstairs lounges. Cover charges vary throughout the night, but come in a pair of tennis shoes and you won't even get that far.

226 W. Ontario
(312) 787.4480
Chicago

Y

If Sound-Bar grew up, kicked off its dancing shoes, moved to Beverly Hills and married a multi-millionaire, it might start to look something like Y, the latest from Sound-Bar's creator, Rainer Zach. This "luxury cocktail boutique" is all about lounging, usually on reserved cubes, and blowing a paycheck or two on bottle service with triple-digit tags. If that doesn't deter you however, be aware: it takes a lot more than the $20 cover charge to get through the door. Dress to impress and bring a blonde.

224 W. Ontario
(312) 274.1780
Chicago

Rednofive

Catering to upscale VIP and urban chic crowds simultaneously, Rednofive's sultry bi-leveled nightclub has an open layout that continuously has the twenty-somethings dancing throughout. Open into the early morning hours, Rednofive thoughtfully provides plush couches for breaks from the dance floor to sip on a martini and leave the dancing to the hired professionals for a while. Rednofive caters to both the individual and groups, offering private party options for anything from a fundraiser to a bachelorette party.

440 N. Halsted
(312) 733.6699
Grand

River North 105

Loop

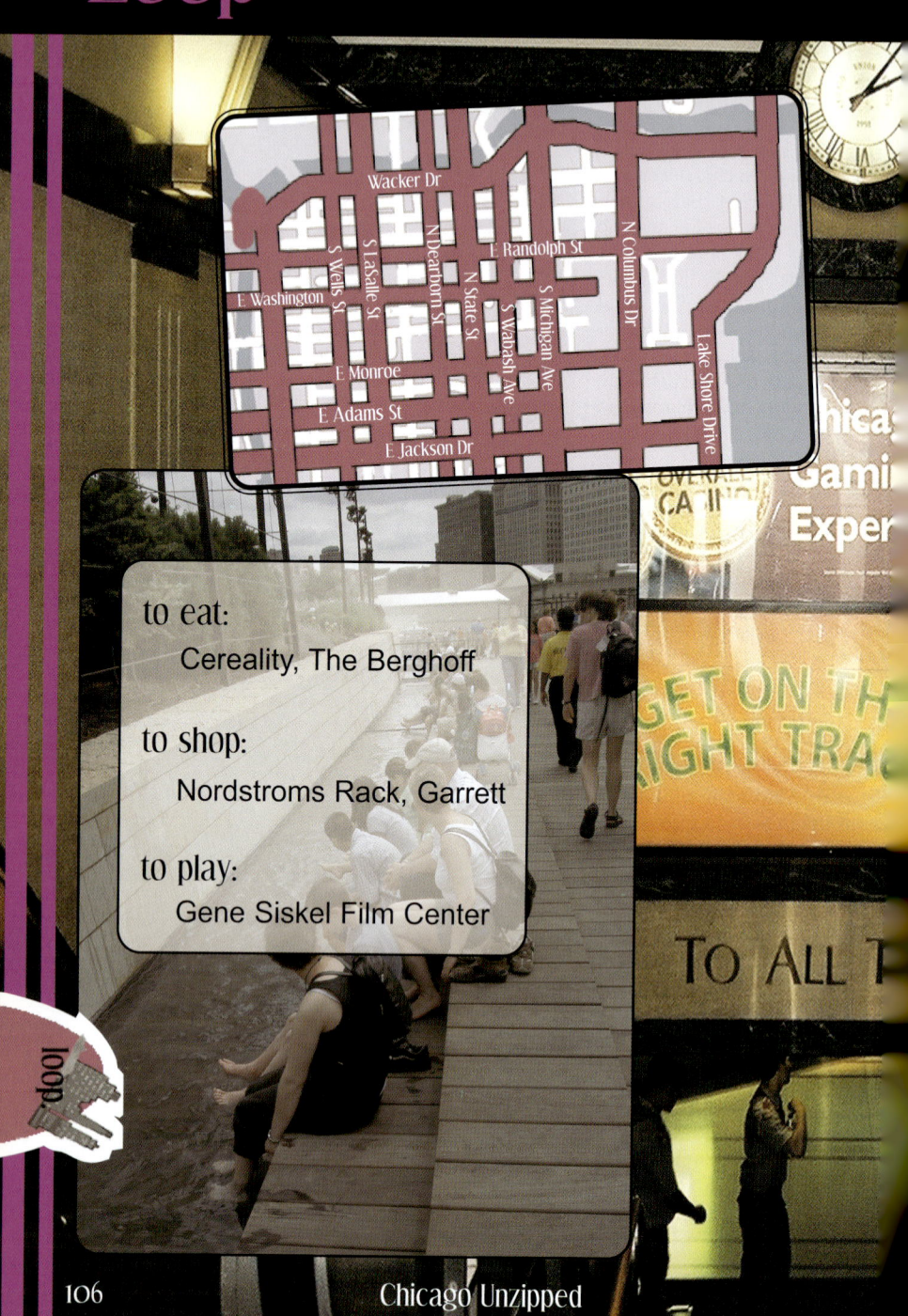

to eat:
   Cereality, The Berghoff

to shop:
   Nordstroms Rack, Garrett

to play:
   Gene Siskel Film Center

Unzipped

Chicago's diverse heart...

In an anatomy of the face of the city, the Loop could be considered Chicago's broken nose. While it's hardly the most glamorous area of the city, the Loop's diverse culture and rich history give it a certain appeal that cannot be found in other areas of downtown.

Here, Chicago is the investment banker leaving the Sears Tower for his lunch break. Here, Chicago is the college student mingling with local blue-collar workers on State Street. Here, Chicago is the artist lingering around the Fine Arts Building or the singer having a drink after a show in the theater district. Here, Chicago is the tourist walking in awe through Grant Park, or looking at her reflection in front of the distorted skyline projected by the bean sculpture. Here, within a few city blocks, the cultural, financial and aesthetic centers of Chicago are all encircled by the el, whose constant roar is like the pulsing beat of the city's heart. Whether you get your kicks from picking up suited businessmen at a bar, dining at a café on the park, or musing over a Monet in the museum, take a tip from Algren and enjoy the Loop as you would an imperfect lover- even if it is just for a one night stand.

www.ChicagoUnzipped.com

to eat.

Treats, BYOB, Pomodoro, Chives, Winds Down, Cereal for Lunch, The Art Institute, Cook

Petterino's

Offering diners a chance to experience the downtown Chicago of the '40s and '50s, Petterino's is the perfect start, or finish, to a night at one of the Loop's theaters. Dark wood and leather accents complement its traditional steakhouse menu, which includes New York strip steak and beef brisket. The prices may be steep, but if using the phrase 'going to the theater" didn't make you feel grown up enough already, being served by the tuxedoed waiters will definitely do the trick.

150 N. Dearborn
(312) 422.0150
Washington

The Italian Village

With three sister restaurants all in one building, each with a unique atmosphere and menu, The Italian Village really is an offer you can't refuse. For a fine-dining experience, go to the street-level restaurant Vivere, with a sleek dining room and contemporary Italian menu. For a more intimate setting, the lower-level restaurant La Cantina special- izes in steak and seafood. Upstairs, The Village-Chicago's oldest Italian restaurant, has a traditional Northern Italian menu with the elaborate setting of a 19th century Italian village.

51 W. Monroe
(312) 332.7005
Monroe

7 on State at Marshall Field's

While all the tourists are lunching at Water Tower, the true Chicagoans take their shopping break on the seventh floor of the original Marshall Field's building on State Street. The staff is helpful and friendly as you decide between salads, grilled and deli sandwiches, noodles, and Mexican food. Once you have your meal, take a seat at a window overlooking the theaters on State or along the interior where you can watch shoppers below while basking in the sunlight streaming through the Tiffany stained-glass dome overhead.

**111 N. State,
7th floor**
(312) 781.1000
Lake

The Berghoff

If you are thirsting for a historical experience, head to The Berghoff, where you can drink the same locally-brewed beer that was served at the World's Fair in 1893. This German-

Boulevard Treats

108 Loop

Loop

American restaurant has been open for more than a century, and is a consistent draw for tourists and Loop-area corporate diners who crave sauerkraut or weinerschnitzel on their lunch breaks. The large dining room is casual, and the walls are lined with historic photos.

17 W. Adams
(312) 427.3170
Monroe

To Pho Café

Serving contemporary Vietnamese cuisine quickly and conveniently, To Pho Café is a "fast, fresh and healthy" BYOB restaurant. Its location directly below the Wabash el stop allows local workers and students to swing by for their lunch menu, when the restaurant converts into a fast-food type service. Later in the afternoon the café morphs into a trendy, happy hour, office party spot. As night falls, To Pho Café dims the lights and offers their dinner menu.

19 N. Wabash
(312) 346.7216
Madison/Wabash

Rhapsody

A block away from the Art Institute and sharing a building with the Chicago Symphony Orchestra, Rhapsody attracts a well-cultured, well-dressed crowd. To get a table inside this fine dining restaurant and wine bar, a reservation will be required; the relaxed outdoor garden seating, however, is first come, first serve. The menu changes with the seasons, and the crowds file in and out according to the symphony performances.

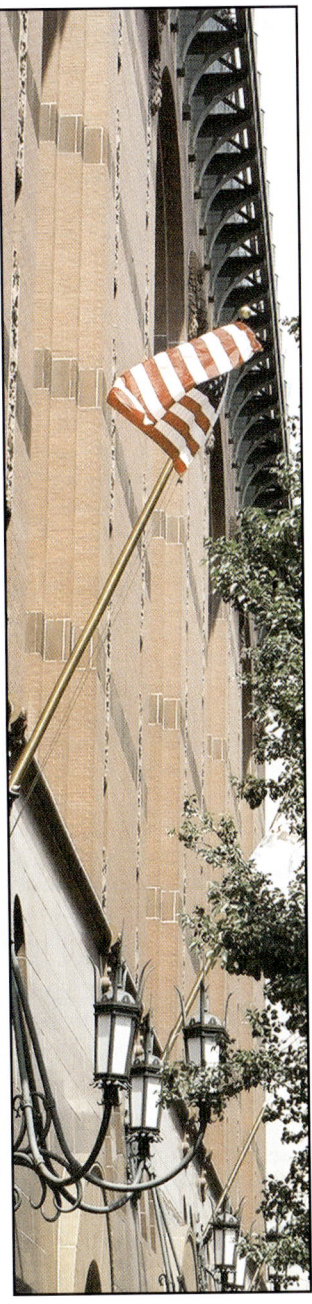

65 E. Adams
(312) 786.9911
Adams

Boulevard Treats

Come and we'll promise you a double-take. Not just because you're seeing double, but because this is one cheap place to satisfy you hunger. The owners, including a set of twins, keep the old school feel of their eatery with old-fashioned décor and old-fashioned prices. With 75 cent ice cream cones and hotdog deals for just a little over a buck, $5 can take you a long way. Perfect after the money spent on the north half of Michigan Ave.

406 S. Michigan
no phone
Grand

Cliché

Welcome to crepe heaven. A sweet crepe, salty crepe, breakfast or lunch, this place has what you want. Whether you're in the mood for a strawberry cheesecake treat or a ham and Asiago cheese delight, the menu boasts so many options your eyes will go rolling back in your head. For a special and unique taste of Euro-joy, try a chilled crepe wrap, for a little warmer finger food, a panini is never a disappointment.

300 S. Wacker
(312) 341.9810
Quincy/Wells

Rivers

With its lobby location in the Chicago Mercantile Exchange Building, Rivers is a sophisticated, quiet restaurant for lunch on the Chicago River. As the work day winds down, Rivers winds up with throngs of young workers pouring in for happy hour specials. Every Friday afternoon, Rivers features live entertainment at "Rock on the River." The lively crowd, all with suit jackets draped over the backs of chairs, proves that Rivers is the place to be - and you can trust them, they're professionals.

30 S. Wacker
(312) 559.1515
Washington/Wells

South Water Kitchen

With the elegance of a back-bayou mansion and the friendliness of southern hospitality, the South Water Kitchen invites passersby to "come to the table!" The high-priced dishes, indicative of the location just off Michigan Avenue and the Chicago River, are forgotten by customers as they delve into savory home-style cooking. South Water Kitchen glorifies the traditional family meal, and is a great place to stop in while shopping on the Magnificent Mile or before enjoying a show in the nearby theater district.

225 N. Wabash
(312) 236.9300
Lake

Bank One Plaza

The expansive cafeteria features all types of cuisine from sushi to NY style deli. The casual environment welcomes anyone and everyone for a relaxing lunch-from middle schoolers with parents to workers from the financial district. The large mosaic wall, high-shooting fountain and one of the "must-visit" Chicago skyscrapers, the Bank One tower, make this sunken plaza so full in the summer that even the stairs become a welcoming lunch time seat.

21 S. Clark
no phone
Monroe/State

Catch 35

Live piano music floats above diners at Catch 35, loud enough to drown out the neighboring table, and quiet enough to serve as a soundtrack to your private dinner conversation. A prominent dessert display reminds you to save room, followed by fresh cuts of fish in a refrigerated display that warn you might not be able to. The location right on the Chicago River invites you to take a post-dinner stroll among the magnificent surrounding skyscrapers that line the river.

35 W. Wacker
(312) 346.3500
Chicago

Tuffano's Vernon Park Tap

This family-oriented Italian restaurant writes its menus on chalk boards on the wall, and is so comfortable with its neighborhood-style dining that it doesn't even take credit cards. Tuffano's is a favorite spot for locals who have been faithful patrons for generations and appreciate the authentic, non-touristy environment along with the large classic Italian dishes.

1073 W. Vernon Park
(312) 733.3393
UIC-Halsted

Monks Pub

The Medieval Times of burger pubs, Monk's apparently takes its name from the Canterbury Tales character. Heavy wooden doors will likely be opened for you by men in ties whom you barely beat before the lunch rush. Thrust your hand into peanut barrels, but save room for the burgers, which have many options from adding olives or jalapenos to fooling yourself that getting cottage cheese on the side instead of fries will make the thick slab of meat healthy.

205 W. Lake
(312) 357.6665
Lake

Venice Café

Of all the non-chain, cafeteria-style Italian fast food joints available for quick lunches (and there are several), Venice Café does it best. Pick your pasta, pick your sauce or choose between sandwich versions of chicken or eggplant parmesan; with any option it's hard to go wrong to satisfy your Italian craving. TVs and permission to smoke cigars adds to the popularity among the after-work crowd, many of whom come from the nearby Mercantile Exchange.

250 S. Wacker
(312) 382.0300
Quincy/Wells

Perry's

Chicago's version of a NY deli serves sandwiches of huge proportions as bewildering as the rest of the dining experience. A cow sign on the front window pokes fun of the "Cows on Parade" relics, random tabloids are framed on the wall, and the owner has been known to harass people on cell phones and play impromptu trivia games. Expect a long line during the lunch rush, but pray it makes your appetite grow enough to tackle the enormous sandwiches.

180 N. Franklin
(312) 372.7557
Clark/Lake

Trattoria No. 10

Why yes, it does feel like there are nearly a dozen trattorias in town, but No. 10 will surprise you. Sneak past street level chain restaurants downstairs to an upscale Italian restaurant that manages to provide interesting combinations of fresh, regional ingredients with comfort trademark dishes. Prices are reasonable for food that dazzles, and the management goes out of their way to ensure a good dining experience. Get drinks at the bar with an early evening buffet to sample the food.

10 N. Dearborn
(312) 984.1718
Washington

Max's Take Out

The epitome of a hole-in-the-wall, this fast food joint is sizzling with delicious flavor. Whether it's a grease fix you need or a quick breakfast or lunch, this place gives you speed and good food for minimal bucks. Convince yourself the egg combos are healthy or indulge in French toast. Grab a stool whose logo suggests you try some Vienna Beef. Popular among working and wandering locals, this is a great downtown favorite kept on the DL.

415 S. Dearborn
(312) 553.0170
Jackson/State

Cereality Cereal Bar & Cafe: This trendy new spot recently debuted in Chicago, offering over 30 different types of cereals and an equally impressive list of toppings. Of course, for this exceptional breakfast extravaganza, multiple types of milk are also available; so lactose-intolerant, have no fear! Proper attire seems to be what you would wear to the breakfast table in your own place, and to make you feel more comfortable in this unconventional scene, the servers also will be wearing pajamas.
100 S. Wacker (312) 506.0010 **Monroe/State**

to shop. Loop

p, A Steal, The Lone Cowboy, Sevens on Sale, Caramel Covered,

Harrison Snack Shop

Join the Columbia College crowd for some quick food and good deals. Take a seat in the comfy booths and scan the menu for cheap and filling meals. Whether it's the breakfast foods or burgers you crave, you can't get bored with all of the options. The burger and fries deal of only $3.10 manages to edge out McDonalds. It's hard to avoid the shop's real hot item; watch out for stampedes to buy cigarettes at the counter.

63 E. Harrison
(312) 341.1270
Harrison

Antiques on Michigan

Urban Outfitters may be selling items that look funky and one-of-a-kind, but for something truly original, look no further than this closet-sized antique store. The jewelry is the real hidden treasure in this store, and trying it on is reminiscent of playing dress up with your grandmother's costume gems. The rest of the store is a collection of odds and ends and even though it looks like something you'd find in your attic, they are all restored to gift-giving quality.

404 S. Michigan
(312) 922.9440
Jackson/State

Nordstrom Rack: As big box retail stores go, this discount Nordstrom outlet is a gift wrapped in a big red bow. Spend hours browsing through the two stories of brand-name clothes, shoes, jewelry and houseware. From Ralph Lauren and Calvin Klein to Blue Cult and Puma, items are marked down as much as 75 percent off, so there is little chance you will leave this store empty-handed. The empty wallet, however, will be your own fault.
24 N. State (312) 377.5500 **Washington/State**

The Garrett Popcorn Shop: With four Chicago locations, Garrett Popcorn Shop has been a Chicago favorite since 1949. Garrett's cheddar cheese and caramel popcorn mix is the most unlikely, yet most popular purchase. Whether walking down State Street, taking a lunch break in Millennium Park, or just in need of a pick-me-up, there's no excuse needed for this American classic snack.
2 W. Jackson (312) 360.1108 **Jackson**

Millenium Park

At a time when some were concerned with Y2K, Chicago was abuzz with plans for Millennium Park, and while the computer bug fizzled, the park has flourished. As the park focuses on modern technology, a free walking tour is available for download onto an MP3 player. The 24.5 acre park's original intention was to hide the railroad tracks that contributed to Chicago's economic rise and aesthetic decline, but the theme of modernity has created a park that, with the Jay Pritzker Pavilion, literally crowns Chicago. With its seating capacity of 7,000 and overhead steel rails contributing to acoustics, the pavilion's amphitheater would be impressive even without architect Frank Gehry's distinctive billows that contribute to the city's skyline despite topping out at 120 feet.

You don't have to be too familiar with Gehry to also recognize the BP bridge that links Millennium Park to the Daley Bicentennial Park as his. The beautiful steel slopes combine function with form as they block out street noise.

Summertime childish giggles with direct you to Crown Fountain, two 50 foot glass towers that project changing Chicago faces underneath cascades of water that creates a shallow pool that begs to be walked through. Periodically the faces will purse their digital lips and fountains will project, spit-like, from the towers. Chicagoans love their nicknames, much to the dismay of sculptor Anish Kappor, whose 110 ton elliptical "Cloud Gate" has been dubbed "The Bean." The sculpture is one of the largest of its kind and thrives on interaction. Check out the reflection of Chicago's skyline, Millennium Park, or yourself as you walk under the 12 foot "gate" at the base. With the former meat packing industry to the south, the Bean finally rounds out Chicago's diet.

If art's your thing, or if you're just looking for a way to celebrate one of Chicago's rare sunny days, Millennium Park offers hours of outdoor entertainment. And if you start to overdose on culture, you can always blow off some steam with some non-adult fun at the ice skating rink.

55 N Michigan, (312) 742.5222

to play.

...chemist, The Right Spot, Modern Swank, Dive Bar, Viola, Buzz, Cubbies Game, Canadia...

to try something else.

Chicago Public Library/ Harold Washington Library

You might swear finals week will be the last time you ever set foot inside a library, but it's still good to know where one is. But let's make this simple: Chicago's main public library, named for Chicago's only African-American mayor, is the largest public library in the world. It's there, it's large, it's the library.

Class dismissed.

400 S. State
(312) 747.4300
Jackson/State

The Symphony Center

The Chicago Symphony Center makes its experience refreshingly available for all budget sizes. The Civic Symphony, for example, is the only training orchestra affiliated with a major American orchestra, and is open to the public free of charge during their season from September to June. More affluent symphony fans can catch the world-renowned Chicago Symphony Orchestra, with tickets ranging from $25-$125, and with student tickets available for most shows.

220 S. Michigan
(312) 294.3000
Jackson/State

Gene Siskel Film Center

While a large popcorn comes in a box barely wide enough for a hand, the movies are what make the experience. Laughing in the face of megaplexes are the small screening rooms that show festival favorites. Beyond the opportunity to catch movies that are often awarded but only show up on video, special events include Q&A sessions with directors and actors after film screenings as well as series covering everything from Mexican silent films to director retrospectives.

164 N. State
(312) 864.2800
State/Lake

Cultural Center

If you are looking to expand your artistic horizons beyond the Art Institute and Museum of Contemporary Art, stop by the galleries at the Chicago Cultural Center. Admission is free as the center is owned by the City of Chicago and the crowd is sparse, which makes viewing an exhibition here a personal, unique experience.

78 Washington
(312) 744.6630
Washington

Minute Massage

True to its name, a massage here can be scheduled as a 10 minute addition to a lunch break, or replace the lunch break entirely with a 90 minute session. Catering to professionals working in the financial district, Minute Massage works only while they work, following a business hours and a weekday schedule. Offering packages up to 1000 minutes, divided as the gift recipient likes, Minute Massage understands the need for squeezing relaxation into the workday.

214 W. Van Buren
(312) 986.1516
Lasalle/Van Buren

114 LOOP

Loop

...ibs, The W, Do You Want More, Lady, **Loop**, A Little to the left, Chicago

to bar hop.

Elephant & Castle Pub and Restaurant

The dark wood and stained glass lighting make this British pub feel like an old boys' club where men in ties sit together drinking whiskey and scotch, but will always offer a lady a light to her cigarette. Primarily an after work watering hole, the Elephant & Castle has a selection of 16 imported beers and a menu of authentic pub-style meals and appetizers. If you are alone, order the fish and chips at the bar.

111 W. Adams
(312) 236.6656
Monroe/State

The Grillroom Chophouse and Wine Bar

A night at the theater would not be complete without a classy dinner for two. If you are looking for a safe bet for you and your date, or just have a hankering for steak, head over to the Grillroom Chophouse and Wine Bar, located front and center of Chicago's theater district. The restaurant's sleek, dark interior is classy, but not too formal, and the steaks and Asian fusion entrees are consistent and sure to complete any night on the town.

33 W. Monroe
(312) 960.0000
Monroe/State

Miller's Pub

Open seven days a week, Miller's Pub offers a restaurant and bar version of Seven Eleven's convenience and the regulars gobble it up every day. With large neon signs and autographed photographs lining the walls, the bar exudes Chicago pride and embodies the comfort of a Midwestern city. The tables are occupied by customers casually enjoying the famous Canadian BBQ ribs, while the bars are lined with sports fans watching games on multiple TVs.

134 Wabash
(312) 263.4988
Monroe/State

Encore

Encore calls itself a Liquid Lounge, and just as it dresses up drinking in the middle of the day, it also dresses up the menu quite nicely. Even the coleslaw is "Wasabi slaw." The menu is complete with the usual upscale salads with simple twists, like the addition of shrimp to a barbeque salad. Flipping over the menu reveals an equal amount of low-carb items in case you're allotting calories to martinis rather than bread.

171 W. Randolph
(312) 338.3788
Chicago

Big Herm's

On the entryway to an old stone building overlooking the river, men in casual Friday attire hoot and holler at co-workers hurling bean bags into wooden targets. Beer cans are served in icy buckets guzzled in the sun that makes Big Herm's come alive from the hot dog joint it is in winter months. The food is greasy and secondary to the after work beer that starts flowing around 3 p.m. on a pretty afternoon.

409 W. Washington
(312) 559.0081
Bus: 29, 56, 65, 66

Spy Bar

Don't let the somewhat creepy alleyway entrance (dumpsters included) fool you, Spy Bar is all about modern swank. After entering on street-level, guests are ushered down a flight of stairs to the trendy underground lounge where $200 bottle service, Hypnotiq martinis and attractive club-goers dancing to hip-hop and house music add to the VIP feel of the velvet furnishings. Just remember to dress to impress and bring cab fare-the few blocks to the el's brown line feel like miles after a few drunken hours in stilettos.

646 N. Franklin
(312) 587.8779
Chicago

The Living Room in The W Hotel City Center

If you're looking for a unique lounge experience, try the trendy Living Room in The W Hotel City Center. Located in the hotel's gothic style lobby, the lounge's Zen-like aura is complete with modern furnishings and DJs who spin from a balcony overlooking the room. Not a great choice for those with shallow pockets or less-than-legitimate ID's, the lounge is more geared toward those with at least a few years of dorm-free living under their belts.

172 W Adams
(312) 917.5608
Quincy/Wells

Manhattan's

If you've always wanted to bring a lawyer home to mom and dad, this is the place to start searching, as it is located near law schools and the financial district. It's not just the cozy atmosphere that makes this bar a favorite, but both the staff and clientele are abnormally good looking. Whether coming from a long day at work or an even longer day of libraries and class, this place has the intimate feel that helps anybody wind-down.

415 S. Dearborn
(312) 957.0460
Jackson/State

Hard Drive

A wall-less bar wonder within the central courtyard

Chicago Public Libr

116 LOOP

Cafe Spot

Artist's Café: Like flies attracted to the cafe's large fluorescent sign, everyone from locals and tourists to art students and big-name performers flock to the Artist's Café. With a gorgeous view of Grant Park, this is the place to eat breakfast al fresco on a sunny morning, or enjoy a late-night beer or cappuccino in an indoor booth. The food, which has kept patrons coming to this restaurant for more than 40 years, is diner-style American, but the menu also includes rotating selection of international specials.
412 S. Michigan (312) 939.7855 **Jackson/State**

Jubilee Juice: Addicts beware: the waffle fries at this joint are harder to swear off than chocolate, booze, or drugs. Showing off an enormous menu that could take hours to peruse, rumor has it the chicken sandwiches are a "not-to-miss." With options ranging from health foods to juicy burgers, no one will be left hungry. Don't miss out on the smoothies, quoted as being "the best in town," or a tasty glass of fresh squeezed juice.
140 N. Halsted
(312) 491.8500
Clinton

Got Pizza Music Cafe: Take a breather from beastly stacked Chicago style slices and enjoy some New York style thin crust pies. Watch your pizza get made before your eyes with the fresh and original ingredients of your choice. With five downtown locations, this place is a great stop for either breakfast or dinner, proving the Bagel Bites commercial right. The common favorite, the Malibu, is a ranchy delight that can be enjoyed to the rhythm of the funky-beats rocking this joint.
719 S. State (312) 957-1111 **Harrison**

of the Hyatt Regency Hotel, Hard Drive makes dancing and people watching easy. Dance around the central fountain and between the fabric columns. Although the lines can be excessively long, it helps to have the right name with VIP standing, which you can call ahead to assure. Treat your eyes to ogling the stunning regulars while treating your belly to some delicious drinks and late-night munchies.

151 E. Wacker
(312) 239.4544
Chicago

to club.

Rumba

Not recommended for its dining experience, Rumba can still offer an outrageous drinking and dancing affair. None of the conservative Midwestern mumbo-jumbo, this restaurant and night club combo rattles with Cuban excitement. Enjoy live Latin music Tuesday-Sunday nights and become a part of the Puerto Rican, Cuban, and South American atmosphere. We are talking, noise, color, attitude and spice. Although prices may be a little steep, it's the experience that's priceless.

351 W. Hubbard
(312) 222.1226
Merchandise Mart

Loop 117

Goldcoast & Streeterville

to eat:
 Grand Lux Cafe, Buca di Beppo, Cactus

to shop:
 Diesel, Ghiradelli, Urban Outfitters

to play:
 Tavern on Rush, Museum of Contemporary Art

118   Chicago Unzipped

Unzipped

Our piece of NYC...

Second only to New York City's Upper East Side when it comes to wealthy city neighborhoods, the Gold Coast will wow you even as you fly down Lake Shore Drive. Well preserved mansions scream old money, while the luxury high rises aren't too cheap either. Since real estate is all about location, location, location, it's no wonder so many of Chicago's must-see attractions are just blocks from the lake views.

The "Magnificent Mile" of Michigan Avenue makes Streeterville Illinois' highest revenue generating strip, but its origins are awash in good old fashioned Chicago scandal. When "Cap" Streeter's steamboat ran aground on a sandbar off E. Superior St. in 1886, Streeter claimed the shallow waters as his own personal territory. Trouble arose when landfills connected Chicago to Streeter's shanty (which is now home to the John Hancock building), which ole "Cap" had filled with alcohol and prostitutes to entertain visitors to the World's Columbian Exposition. Although he lost lawsuits and even shot at cops, it was only Streeter's death in 1921 that finally enabled Chicago to expand into Streeterville. Now home to hyperbolic amusements such as some of the priciest boutiques, highest skyscrapers, most prominent museums, and Chicago's most popular and child-friendly Navy Pier, Streeterville still entertains out-of-town visitors, even without prostitution.

goldcoast streeterville.

www.ChicagoUnzipped.com

to eat.

aurant-Riddled, Choice Cuts, Drooling, Hot Spot, Legendary, Eyein' the Waiter, Methi M

Big Bowl

This casual eatery puts a modern spin on traditional Asian fare with wok-tossed creations like Fiery Szechuan Chicken and Thai Basil Shrimp, as well as soups, salads and appetizers. Picky eaters will enjoy the stir fry bar, where diners can fill their own bowl with ingredients from the display of vegetables, meats, sauces, rice and noodles. Those lazy restaurant-goers wishing to stay at their table can also send their server to the bar to fill a bowl with their choice of ingredients.

6 E. Cedar
(312) 640.8888
Clark/Division

Morton's, The Steakhouse

Dining at a legendary restaurant's original location is always promising, and Morton's follows through every step of the way. Start with the creamy lobster bisque, but be forewarned you will be hard pressed to find bisque elsewhere that will live up to this precedent. The cartload of steak offerings is sure to satisfy even the most serious of carnivores, and if you have room, dig into the heavenly Godiva hot chocolate cake.

1050 N. State
(312) 266.4820
Clark/Division

Tsunami

Located a block away from restaurant-riddled State Street, Tsunami attracts Chicagoans who know where to look for good sushi. Being off the beaten path provides an intimate rather than commercial atmosphere.

Whether enjoying some of their creative sushi combinations at the sushi bar or sipping their newest sake concoction in the chic sake lounge, you're sure to be impressed by this contemporary Japanese restaurant.

1160 Dearborn
(312) 642.9911
Clark/Division

Burrito Beach

A downtown alternative to Chipotle, Burrito Beach boasts a plethora of overflowing burritos and other Mexican foods. From cheap breakfast burritos and tacos to their famous Baja Chipotle Burrito, any meal can be made Mexican. If you're not too hungry or just want to spice things up, a side of guacamole is this joint's secret weapon. Look to their 4-foot Burrito for an original meeting or party food selection.

200 E. Ohio
(312) 335.0668
Grand

Gibson's Steakhouse

Gibson's will leave you whistling a Sinatra tune not

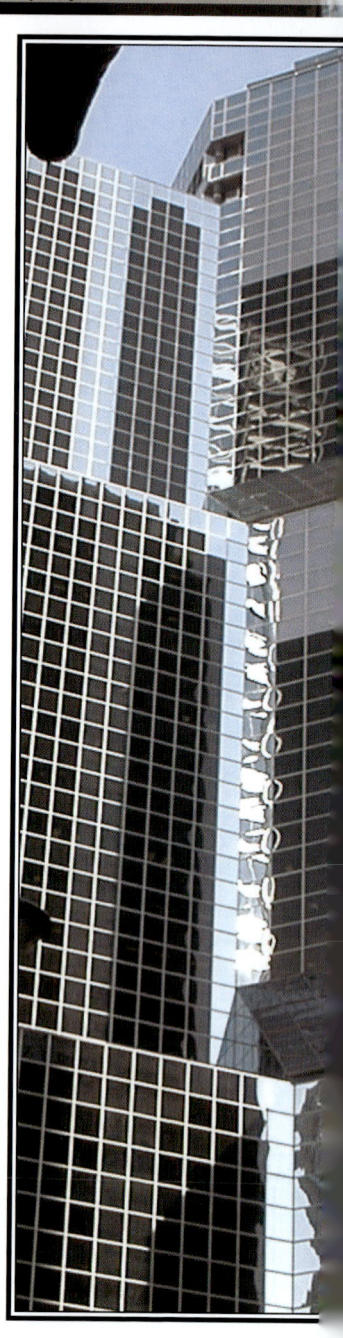

120 Goldcoast & Streeterville

Goldcoast & Steeterville

because of the background music, but because of the old-school Chicago experience. The dining room is loud and lively, and the staff is energetic and engaging as they help you navigate the selection of choice cuts of meats. You can't go wrong with any of the steaks, but make sure someone at the table orders a twice-baked potato: they are legendary and large enough to share.

1028 N. Rush
(312) 266.8999
Clark/Division

Windy City Wraps

In either of its two downtown locations, Windy City wraps are made to order with your choice of four different tortilla styles and a variety of hot and cold ingredients for meat-eaters and vegetarians. All wraps are topped off with a dainty dollop of fresh seasonal fruit and there are a variety of fresh smoothies to wash the food down. Windy City Wraps is small enough to spy the owner walking among the lunch rush, but hip enough to provide internet.

11 E. Ohio
(312) 836.9100
Grand

Emilio's Tapas Sol Y Nieve

Like a bull towards a red cape, Spanish lovers charge towards Emilio's. The outside seating is perfect for the rare Chicago sunny weather and the inside is decorated with beautiful Spanish murals and tile mosaics all highlighted by classic Spanish music. Although a bit pricey, numerous culinary awards and various hot and cold tapas dishes validate the cost. Also, the Spanish-speaking waiters are always smiling and eager to help you brush up your Spanish.

215 E. Ohio
(312) 467.7177
Grand

Bandera

Order the chicken. Even when you realize it's actually one of the less expensive entrees, don't doubt its quality. Put down the menu and order the chicken. Thanks to its atmosphere, Bandera doesn't feel like the corporate chain restaurant it is. Within the dark, intimate dining room, its table linens are offset by cowhide upholstery, meaning it's nice enough to take a date, but relaxed enough to stop in after a day of shopping on Michigan Ave. Yee haw.

535 N. Michigan
(312) 644.3524
Grand

Grand Lux Café

The Grand Lux might as well be called Le Grand Cheesecake-it bears a striking resemblance to its sister restaurant-but truth be told, that's also what makes the Lux so damn good. With the same gargantuan portions, novel-length menu and décor that differ only in the Café's Venetian flair, you might experience a moment of déjà vu. While you may appreciate the subtle differences between the two restaurants, don't be surprised if you are left craving cheesecake at the end.

600 N. Michigan
(312) 276.2500
Grand

Johnny Rocket's

Just like in real estate, the key to a successful late-night diner is location, location, location. Steps from the bars, Johnny Rocket's burgers, fries and BLT's are sure to satisfy the most drunken of 2 a.m. munchies. One other perk: the servers wear those little white paper cook's hats circa 1950, and if you are nice they will probably give you one, too. Because, let's be honest, in your intoxicated haze, you'll think you'd look pretty hot in that hat.

901 N. Rush
(312) 377.3900
Chicago

The Signature Room

Touting what is undoubtedly "the view of the city," this restaurant on the 95th floor of the John Hancock Building is an instant Chicago classic. The million-dollar view does come with a price, but the food is as good as the atmosphere, whether you order the salmon filet or the rack of lamb. If you are looking for a steal, make reservations for the Saturday lunch buffet, only $18 for adults, compared to Sunday's $37.50 brunch.

875 N. Michigan
(312) 787.9596
Grand

Lawry's Prime Rib

There are no secret recipes at this spice giant's restaurant, but you can see for yourself how a little Lawry's seasoned salt can go a long way. Housed in the McCormick Mansion that dates back to the 1890s, the elegant atmosphere at Lawry's tops off an already incredible dining experience. As the name suggests, prime rib is king, with six different cuts all topped off with Lawry's famous whipped horseradish sauce.

100 E. Ontario
(312) 787.5000
Grand

Weber Grill

A restaurant affiliated with a famous line of outdoor cooking ranges-genius. You know they must take their grilling seriously here, and your meal will probably leave you wanting to order a new Weber grill for yourself at the end of your meal. Even the patio is fenced in with grill tops. Whatever you order, make sure it's drenched in barbecue sauce, because their blend is better than anything you've ever used in your backyard.

539 N. State
(312) 467.9696
Grand

Rosebud on Rush

You won't have a hard time finding this restaurant, as the sign's trademark rosebud illuminates a dark corner of Rush Street, beckoning patrons to this classic Italian experience. This is another restaurant known as a Chicago celebrity hub, as famous faces flock here to enjoy the selection of high quality meats as well as the

Lake Shore Drive

chef's homemade "square noodles," or the chicken vesuvio.

720 N. Rush
(312) 266.6444
Chicago

Le Colonial

A pricey place for special occasions or impressing a date, Le Colonial serves fine dining with multiple courses. The sign out front immediately reminds potential customers that "proper attire is required," and reservations are recommended for this hot spot surrounded by other equally popular destinations for later in the night. The exotic Vietnamese cuisine and alluring upstairs lounge attract stylish cosmopolites from all reaches of the city.

871 N. Rush
(312) 266.1414
Chicago

Service Entrance Deli & Catering

Appear to know Chicago inside and out by bringing an out-of-towner off Michigan Avenue, through a random alleyway behind the John Hancock building, and get buzzed into a delightfully hidden deli. Patronize the food courts of the Magnificent Mile no more after discovering a deli that lets you create your own sandwich or save with half portions. While the secret location is cool, it's the delicious sandwiches that make it a favorite and a caterer.

215 E. Chestnut
(312) 787.4525
Chicago

Amarit

Downtown dining needn't always be fancy or expensive. Amarit is located close enough to Michigan Ave. and Rush St. to provide a break from shopping, but far enough away from the hubbub to feel like a neighborhood gem. Make Amarit your new favorite Thai restaurant by ordering a bubble tea latte or any of the entrees priced at $6.25, and stay authentic by trying a Thai beer.

1 E. Delaware
(312) 649.0500
Chicago

Luciano's on Rush: With its prominent sign on the south tip of Rush Street, this Italian restaurant looks promising. Inside, the pseudo-Tuscan décor is a little generic, but the atmosphere is helped greatly by the live music. (The nightly music is called a "cabaret," but isn't nearly as exotic as the word suggests). The food is basic but affordable, including favorites like the gnocchi or rigatoni with pancetta. **871 N. Rush** (312) 266.1414 Chicago

Tempo

This pleasant breakfast restaurant that would make your grandparents proud on Sunday afternoons will still be there for you at 5 a.m. after partying on Rush. Their full breakfast menu is offered 24 hours, with some patrons starting and ending their evening over pancakes or an omelet. As one worker observes, "Some people get meaner after they drink, some people get nicer, and that's life." With inexpensive items and a great location, expect a long but worthwhile wait.

6 E. Chestnut
(312) 943.4373
Chicago

Boston Blackie's

When asked, the manager couldn't say what makes these amazing burgers claim a Boston origin. Everything is thick at Blackie's, from the juicy burgers to steak fries - even the salads are daunting with names including the word "garbage." The swank of the Gold Coast location is fitting, the Loop location offers a lunch hot spot or a place for after-work beers, and locations in the suburbs are still relished.

164 E. Grand
(312) 938.8700
Grand

Buca di Beppo

Bringing new meaning to family-style Italian dining, the décor is your Italian grandmother's house, furniture and all, and you can even eat at the kitchen table with a reservation. Garlic lovers should start with the cheesy garlic bread, made with whole cloves of garlic, and those looking for a more mild kick should stick with the bruschetta. All the pastas are great, but if you are looking for something different, the chicken marsala is syrupy sweet and amazing.

2941 N. Clark
(773) 348.7673
Wellington

Phil Stefani's 437 Rush

With the Phil Stefani name attached, it's no surprise this Italian steakhouse doesn't miss a beat. The steaks have been marinated in sauces for more than 20 days, and the seafood is light and flavorful. As far as the atmosphere goes, it can feel more like a place to have a business lunch than a place to have a date. But no matter what the reason you choose to dine here, you are sure to enjoy it.

437 N. Rush
(312) 222.0101
Grand

Gino's on Rush

When it comes to Chicago-style pizza, everyone has an opinion. While there will never be a definitive deep-dish victor, Gino's is a strong, often underrated contender. The flaky, cornbread-sweet crust adds to the flavor of the pizza, without getting a soggy, doughy consistency (pizza analysis is a science, if you haven't noticed). The restaurant itself also has more of an old-school neighborhood feel than other nearby deep-dish eateries-the walls are etched with names of regulars and tourists alike.

633 N. Wells
(312) 943.1124
Chicago

Albert's Café & Patisserie

The delicious combination of a café and a Patisserie recreates the feel of a casual afternoon in Paris. With only 10-15 small tables, Albert's offers a cozy setting for any meal or snack, especially breakfast and lunch. In the spirit of rich French cooking, the menu assures customers that all cookies are made with 100% butter and all drinks are served with only premium liquors. You may hear of their famous wedding cakes, but come prepared to be tempted by a meal.

52 W. Elm
(312) 751.0666
Clark/Division

Roy's

Aloha can mean goodbye Chicago winter, hello Hawaiian-fusion. With more than 30 other Roy's restaurants in the country, it's true that dining here is not necessarily unique, however the menu's blend of Pacific Rim, French and Japanese flavors is a rare find in the Chicago dining scene. So if you are looking for an upscale dining experience but are over the steakhouse scene, Roy's is sure to hit the spot.

720 N. State
(312) 787.7599
Chicago

Merlot on Maple

As a general rule, this restaurant falls into the "big guns" category: unless you've recently won the lottery or been drafted to the Bulls, reserve it for proposals and I-cheated-on-you-confession dinners only. That being said, Merlot on Maple is a beautiful restaurant with beautiful food and beautiful servers with beautiful Italian accents. Authentic Bolognaise cuisine complements an elegant atmosphere created by dark wood and ivory table linens, sure to impress even the most reluctant of dates-or potential fiancés.

16 W. Maple
(312) 335.8200
Clark/Division

Billy Goat Tavern

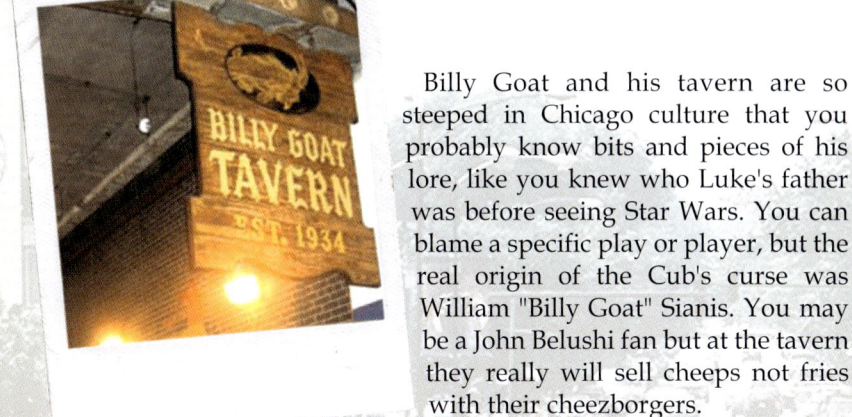

Billy Goat and his tavern are so steeped in Chicago culture that you probably know bits and pieces of his lore, like you knew who Luke's father was before seeing Star Wars. You can blame a specific play or player, but the real origin of the Cub's curse was William "Billy Goat" Sianis. You may be a John Belushi fan but at the tavern they really will sell cheeps not fries with their cheezborgers.

You can go to the Billy Goat Tavern offshoot in the Loop, but the subterranean bar hidden underneath the Magnificent Mile is the real deal. Billy Goat Sianis has been hailed as the city's best tavern keeper, and fans of clubs and bars could learn from the master. Whether publicity stunt or actual quirk, Sianis loved his pet goat (more loyal than a dog and you can always milk or eat a goat) and brought him everywhere . . . hospital rooms, public events, but it was being barred from the World Series Game that will cost the Cubs the pennant every year.

The Sianis and Belushi families were friends, and Second City alum John Belushi made the tavern famous in a Saturday Night Live skit. Doubters of Billy Goat Tavern's greatness need only look so far as the tavern's walls, which are plastered with yellowed newspaper articles boasting the greatness of the place.

Goldcoast & Streeterville 125

to shop.

...pagne, Shimmer, Shells, Chocolate Twist, Human-Sized Hershey's Kiss, Cheap Thrills, Poo...

PS: Accessories

This intimate boutique might remind you of what you could only hope your closet would look like: a small space crammed with shoes, purses, jewelry, and other accessories (jeweled bras and undies included). Other pluses include surprisingly reasonable prices, meaning that the usual rule of small store and small selection equals huge prices does not apply, unique beaded jewelry and friendly sales people. Accessory hounds will be in heaven. Fortunately, those with a smaller bank account can still afford groceries after a visit.

1127 N. State
(312) 932.0077
Clark/Division

PUMA Store Chicago

The PUMA Store Chicago brings hip culture to sport culture in their newest North American location. Upon entering the store, complete with white walls and brand signature red accents, shoppers are met by conveniently placed models (if you're lucky, you'll even get a hello from the one holding the bike by the entrance) and a DJ spinning. There are two stories of anything and everything PUMA, including three full walls of shoes, sure to satisfy both fashion and sports fans alike.

1051 N. Rush
(312) 751.8574
Clark/Division

NYLA

If you're looking for cheap thrills, you're in the wrong place, but deep-pocketed fashion followers will appreciate this very trendy, coast-to-coast boutique. Hard-to-find denim labels like Rock and Republic and People for Peace line the shelves, while racks of men's and women's tops and bottoms fill the rest of the retail space. And while prices run mostly in the triple digits, friendly sales people, not to mention the 50 percent off racks in the back, help buffer the immediate shock.

1133 N. State
(312) 280.8398
Grand

Ghirardelli Soda Fountain and Chocolate Shop

Though Ghirardelli is a mainstay tourist attraction at Water Tower, this is more than a run-of-the-mill chocolate souvenir shop. No matter what the season, you will find a gourmet chocolate delicacy to satisfy your sweet tooth. The hot chocolate will keep you warm in sub-zero winds and it tastes like a chocolate bar melted in warm milk. On a summer day, cool off with one of their rich, icy

Goldcoast & Steeterville

milkshakes made with your choice of ice cream flavors.

830 N. Michigan
(312) 337.9330
Chicago

Chalet Wine & Cheese

Don't let the $50 and up bottles in the entryway scare you, near the back $5.99 bottles of champagne sit next to Veuve Cliquot. The staff is eager to help with your wine selection, as indicated by the shelf of "Wine for Dummies" type books. The front of the store offers a deli stocked with meat, cheese, caviar, truffles, or whatever delicacy you choose to pair with your wine to treat your refined palate.

40 E. Delaware
(312) 787.8555
Chicago

Potash Bros. Supermart

This organic market of the city offers quality groceries at affordable prices. Stop by and make a salad to go, or order a sandwich from the deli as an alternative to restaurants while you pick up specialty items. Sealing the deal, deli meat is roasted on premises and groceries can be delivered if you're feeling lazy but still want to support independent grocers who have been around since 1950.

1525 N. Clark
(312) 337.7537
Clark/Division

The Hershey Company

When rival confectioner Hershey set up a shop close to chocolate magnate Ghirardelli, more than a few eyebrows were raised. But Ghirardelli fans can rest easy, because the Hershey Store pales in comparison. More specifically, walking into the Hershey Store is like watching the candy aisle of a grocery store throw up in a Toys R Us. Between its gaudy décor, gimmicky chocolate-dispensing machine, and generic treats, even a sweet tooth could get a headache.

822 N. Michigan
(312) 337.7711
Chicago

Tails in the City

Has Paris Hilton's Tinkerbell made your puppy jealous? Treat your pooch to a "chewy vuitton," a faux Juicy tube dress, or any of the ridiculous accessories lining the walls. This boutique really has gone to the dogs, from the pastries that look good enough for humans to bottled dog water. Cats are not neglected with a wall filled with gourmet catnip and the like. Even non-animal lovers should take a peek inside to see that these indulgences really exist.

1 E. Delaware
(312) 649.0347
Chicago

MCA Store

to play.

to try something else.

Museum of Contemporary Art: First Fridays

On the first Friday of every month the Museum of Contemporary Art hosts a party for anyone interested in walking around the museum with martinis, while making creative interpretations of modern art. Among an abundance of appetizers, singletons with success stories mingle, checking each other out as much as the art. The swanky party demands an after-party, so as reliable as their art work is original, the MCA sponsors an after-party at varying Chicago bars following the close of the museum at 10 p.m.

220 E. Chicago
(312) 280.2660
Chicago

Navy Pier

Beyond the tourists, Navy Pier holds secrets for low-budget entertainment options. A free trolley runs along the pier, a perfect ride for a view of the area and free transportation to the el. Climbing to the top floor of the parking structure gives a dazzling view of the skyline, lakefront and giant Ferris wheel. The indoor portion contains the free Smith Museum of Stained Glass Windows. Other more costly but fun options include the numerous restaurants and bars, an IMAX Theater, the Funhouse Maze and vendor shopping.

600 E. Grand
(312) 595.7537
Grand, bus

Astrology Readings by Sara

Proving that the Gold Coast may be predictable (literally), but never boring, Sara's horoscope readings are actually done in her home. Watching TV with her family as you wait may seem odd, but that only adds to the private and personal feel you want from the predictor of your future. In-depth palm reading costs $20, while the quick yet interesting character reading costs only $10. Sara also offers Tarot card readings and past, present, and future guidance.

157 E. Ohio, 3rd Floor
(312)755.1865
Grand

to bar hop.

Tavern on Rush

The bar at this famous steakhouse has a classic feel, but still draws a young, lively crowd. The space is simple - a moderately-sized room where people circulate around bar-top tables to mingle, see, and be seen. An eclectic mix of music plays in the background as groups sip on cocktails, enjoying the novel atmosphere of a bar where you can actually hold a conversation.

1031 N. Rush
(312) 664.9600
Clark/Division

Cru Cafe and Wine Bar

Only the last two pages of the leather bound menu are devoted to food, an indication of what a wine bar really is. Menu items like the cheese and charcuterie platter emphasize the focus on wine, while other items like the "salad tower" are just fun and tasty. The wine bar is meant to initiate rather than intimidate with classes and sampler flights offered. Leather couches by a fire-

128 Goldcoast & Streeterville

Goldcoast & Steeterville

place beckon a bottle of wine whether you know what to taste for or not.

888 N. Wabash
(312) 337.4078
Chicago

The Back Room

State Street restaurants provide the food; the Back Room provides the live entertainment. The Back Room invites anyone over 21 to listen to different local Chicago jazz artists featured nightly. The renowned upstairs VIP room is a popular spot for celebrities and has recently opened for private parties. The downstairs layout is spaciously arranged so there isn't a bad room in the house. Fulfill your two drink minimum with a chocolate martini and their famous jazz martini.

1007 N. Rush
(312) 751.2433
Clark/Division

The Hunt Club

True to its name, this upscale sports bar is full of well-dressed twenty-somethings on the prowl for a fresh piece of meat. While upscale enough to merit a collared shirt, the crowd is laid-back and the drinks are reasonably priced, perhaps inspiring you to buy a few cocktails for someone you meet. If you mingle with anyone interesting, move to the upper level where you can dance to the DJ's music while watching the mating rituals below.

1100 N. State
(312) 998.7887
Clark/Division

Cactus Gold Coast

Mexican food, margaritas, beer, and sports. What more could a young professional ask for in an after work spot? The small interior reminds customers that Cactus is squeezed into the middle of a busy city, but the size doesn't bother the crowd that stands at the bar lost in an Illinois sports game. When the weather warms up, people spill out front into the Mardi Gras bead decorated beer garden.

1112 N. State
(312) 642.5999
Clark/Division

The Bar at The Peninsula

The Peninsula should hire a man to sit at the bar, uniformed in a blue velvet smoking jacket, to puff a tobacco pipe and greet patrons as they walk in-because that's the only thing that could complete the scene at this dark, intimate hotel lounge. The bar's intimate atmosphere is a great place to set the mood for a fancy night on the town, or just to relax with a drink and wander onto the hotel's nearby sky deck to enjoy the city view.

108 Superior
(312) 337.2888
Chicago

Goldcoast & Streeterville 129

Blue Chicago

You don't have to be a blues aficionado to know that as bars go, this one's got soul. The talent at this small venue is unparalleled, and will make a blues fan of anyone. Get there early to snag one of the booths or barstools lining the walls before the bar fills to standing room only. The bartenders are generous and the staff maintains a great door policy so even when the bar fills up, patrons have plenty of room to breathe.

736 N. Clark
(312) 642.6261
Chicago

Whiskey Sky

In case the W's lobby didn't impress you enough with trademark engaging decorations, head up to a breathtaking panoramic view of the city. With nearly floor to ceiling windows that curve out as they go up, the Chicago skyline gets more attention than the beautiful people sipping delicious, pricey drinks. The small space can create both intimacy and a rush for leather seats near the window.

644 N. Lakeshore
(312) 943.9200
Bus: 29, 56, 65, 66

The Underground Wonder Bar

By "underground," they mean underground. And by "wonder" they must mean it's a wonder you can find a bar like this off Rush Street. With its hole-in-the-wall feel and live music, this bar draws a much more eclectic, laid-back crowd than surrounding watering holes. But even with the more alternative, intimate feel, you'll be reminded you are still on the Gold Coast when you shell out a $12 cover for the house band and sit among the older, professional and touristy crowd.

10 E. Walton
(312) 266.7761
Chicago

Jilly's Piano Bar

As a piano bar, Jilly's is hit or miss. The atmosphere feels more like a pick-up scene than a lounge. The music is good, and when the bar fills up, the crowd is pretty lively on the small dance floor. But if you just want to relax with a glass of wine, or talk with a group, get there early, because later on you'll be packed like sardines and won't be able to hear yourself speak.

1007 N. Rush
(312) 664.1001
Clark/Division

Zebra Lounge

If you find yourself a little too tipsy around midnight, but aren't ready to admit defeat yet, come listen to great talent tickle the ivories while you wind down. The lounge is dark and intimate, and the crowd is a mixed bag of older patrons, young party-goers and 30-something Gold Coast yuppies. This is definitely a late night hangout as past 1 a.m., getting a table can be hit or miss, so make sure to stake your claim early enough.

1220 N. State
(312) 642.5140
Clark/Division

to club.

Le Passage

Walking down a velvet-roped alley (the "passage" for which the club is named) and down stairs past a bouncer gives the feeling of leaving one world and entering another. This new red and gold, dimly-lit realm is packed with people dancing to loud music with fancy martinis. Half of the room is occupied by small groups with reserved tables and bottle service. Literally underground yet well known, Le Passage is an expensive and popular place to see and be seen.

937 N. Rush
(312) 255.0022
Chicago

SYN

The intriguing claim of being Chicago's premier discotheque fizzles once you get past the tuxedo-clad doorman, when you realize this underground club is a far cry from Studio 54. If you get an eerie feeling when the DJ plays "We are Family" because it's a little like dancing with mom and dad, don't despair because this means the men are eager to buy younger girls drinks and the women are friendly and unpretentious.

1009 N. Rush
(312) 664.0009
Chicago

Goldcoast & Streeterville 131

to find.

Bucktown/Wicker Park

City website:
www.wickerparkbucktown.com

Area information:
773.384.2672
info@wickerparkbucktown.com

Alderman:
Walter Burnett, Jr., 27th Ward
312-432-1995
wburnett@cityofchicago.org

Police:
13th District
937 N. Wood St.
312-746-8357

Library:
Damen Branch
2056 N. Damen Avenue
312.744.6022

West Town Branch
1310 N. Milwaukee Avenue
773.744.1473

Evanston

City website:
www.cityofevanston.com

City information:
847-328-2100

Police:
1454 Elmwood Avenue
847-866-5000
police@cityofevanston.org

Mayor's Office:
847-866-2979

Civic Center:
2100 Ridge Avenue

Crisis Line:
800-322-8400

Library:
1703 Orrington Avenue
847-866-0300
director@epl.org

Parking Systems:
847-866-2923

Gold Coast

City website:
www.goldcoastneighborhood.com

Alderman:
Burton F. Natarus, 42nd Ward
312-744-3062
bnatarus@cityofchicago.org

Police:
18th District
1160 N. Larrabee Ave.
312-742-5870

Lakeview

City website:
www.lakevieweast.com

Alderman:
Thomas M. Tunney, 44th Ward
773-525-6034
ward44@cityofchicago.org

Police:
23rd District (West)
3600 N. Halsted St.
312-744-8320

19th District (East)
2452 W. Belmont Ave.
312-744-5983

Chamber of Commerce:
3030 N. Broadway
773-348-8608

Lincoln Park

City website:
www.lincolnparkchamber.com

Alderman:
Vi Daley, 43rd Ward
773-327-9111
vdaley@cityofchicago.org

Police:
18th District
1160 N. Larrabee Ave.
312-742-5870

Chamber of Commerce:
2530 N. Lincoln Ave #113
773-880-5200

132 Index

unzipped.

Loop

Alderman:
Madeline L. Haithcock,
2nd Ward
773-924-0014
mhaithcock@cityofchicago.org

Police:
1st District
1718 South State Street
312-745-4290

Old Town

Alderman:
Vi Daley, 43rd Ward
773-327-9111
vdaley@cityofchicago.org

Police:
18th District
1160 N. Larrabee Ave.
312-742-5870

River North

Local website:
rivernorthassociation.com

Alderman:
Burton F. Natarus, 42nd Ward
312-744-3062
bnatarus@cityofchicago.org

Police:
18th District
1160 N. Larrabee Ave.
312-742-5870

Roger's Park

City website:
www.rogerspark.org

Police:
24th District
6464 N. Clark St.
312-744-5907

Alderman:
Joe Moore, 49th Ward
773-338-5796
jmoore@cityofchicago.org

Community Council:
1530 W. Morse Ave
773-338-RPCC
rpcc@rogerspark.org

Library:
6905 N. Clark Street
312-744-7995

Uptown

City website:
www.uptownchicagocommission.org

Alderman:
Helen Shiller, 46th Ward
773-878-4646
ward46@cityofchicago.org

Police:
23rd District (West)
3600 N. Halsted St.
312-744-8320

19th District (East)
2452 W. Belmont Ave.
312-744-5983

City of Chicago

Chicago Office of Tourism
(312) 744-2400
78 E Washington St

www.chicago.il.org

www.cityofchicago.org

www.chicagotraveler.com

Index 133

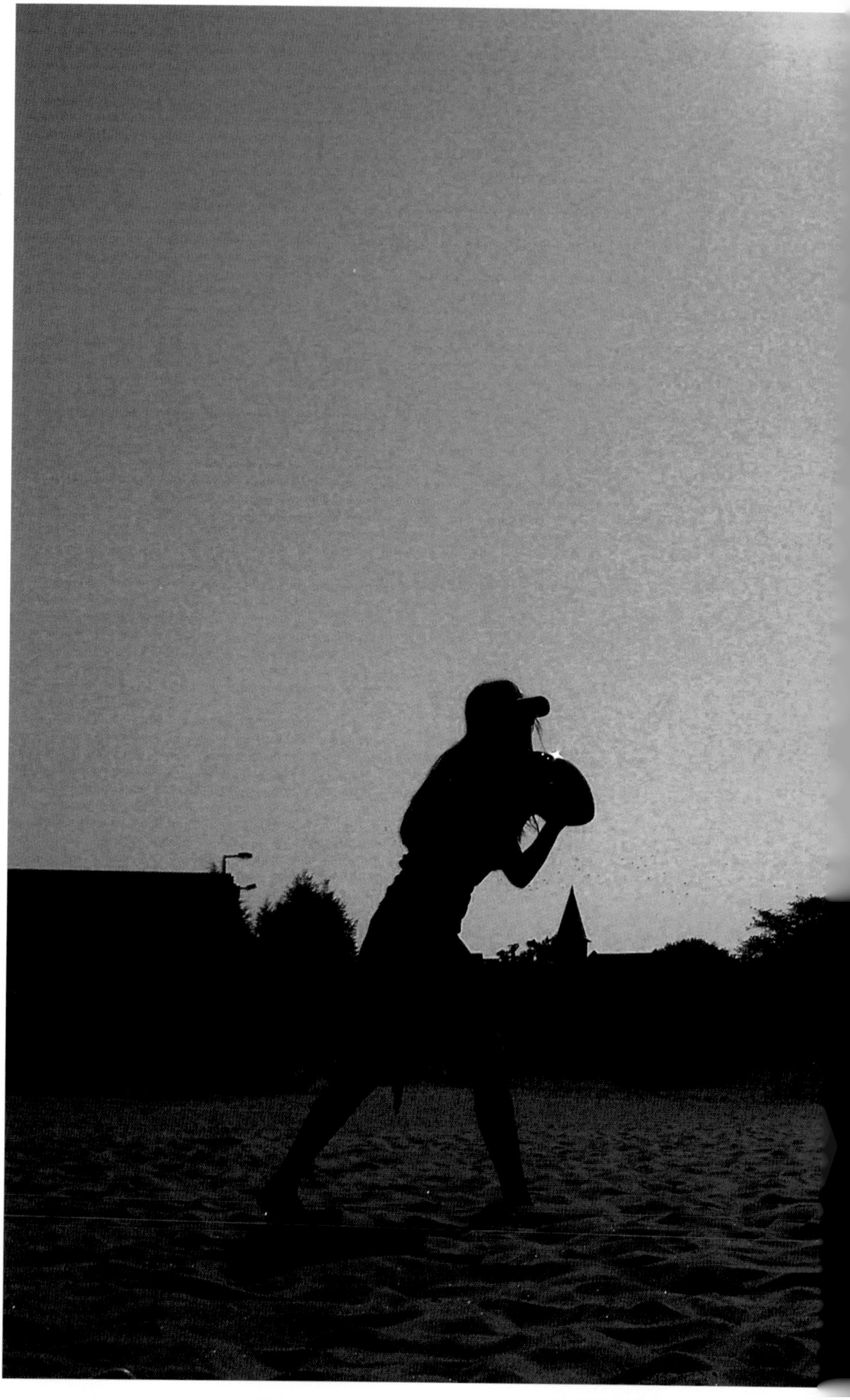

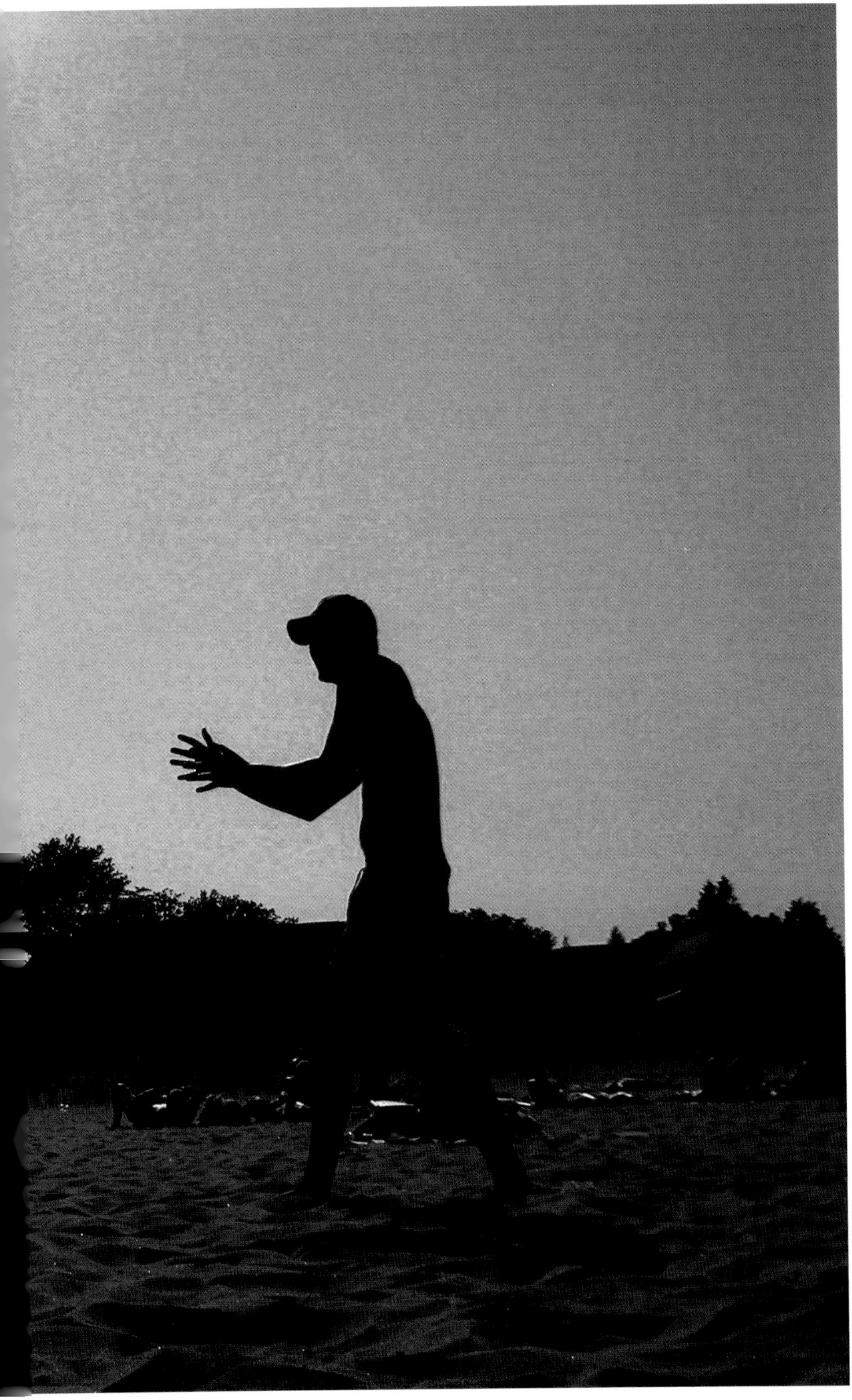

to find.

BWP..... Bucktown/Wicker Park
GC......... Gold Coast
EV........... Evanston
LV........... Lakeview
LP........... Lincoln Park
LO.......... Loop
OT.......... Oldtown
RN.......... River North
RP.......... Roger's Park
UP.......... Uptown

to eat.

American

7 on State, LO, $, 108
Alibi, RN, $$, 96
Al's Italian Beef, RN, $$, 96
Bandera, GC, $$$, 121
Big Herm's, LO, $, 116
Bin 36, RN, $$$, 96
Blue Bayou, LV, $$, 41
Blue Frog Bar and Grill, RN, $$, 94
Bordo's, LP, $$, 66
Boston Blackies, GC, $$, 124
Brett's Kitchen, RN, $$, 95
Bourgeois Pig, LP, $, 56
Cactus, GC, $$, 129
Cereality Cereal Bar, LO, $, 111
Chicago Bagel Authority, LP, $, 57
Chicago Diner, LV, $$, 40
Cliché, LO, $, 109
Cooking Fools, BWP, $$, 72
Crew Bar and Grill, UP, $$, 37
Cru Café & Wine Bar, GC, $$, 128
Dixie Kitchen & Bait Shop, EV, $$, 9
Duke of Perth, LV, $$, 53
Earwax Café, BWP, $, 71
Ed Debevic's, RN, $$, 94
Elephant & Castle, LO, $$, 115
Encore, LO, $$, 116
Ennui Café, RP, $, 17
Fluky's, RP, $, 16

Gepperth's Meat Market, LP, $$$, 57
Gibson's Steakhouse, GC, $$$, 120
Ginbucks, BWP, $$, 73
Gino's on Rush, GC, $$, 124
Giselle's, LP, $$, 57
The Grand Central, LP, $$, 66
Grand Lux Café, GC, $$, 121
Heartland Café, RP, $$, 18
Johnny Rocket's, GC, $, 122
Julius Meinl, LV, $, 41
Karyn's Cooked, RN, $$, 97
Lawry's Prime Rib, GC, $$$$, 122
La Baguette, LV, $, 44
Max's Take Out, LO, $, 111
McDonalds, RN, 100
Melrose Restaurant, LV, $, 43
Melting Pot, RN, $$$, 96
Miller's Pub, LO, $$, 115
Monk's Pub, LO, $, 110
Moonshine, BWP, $$, 80
Moresland, RP, $$, 18
Morton's Steakhouse, GC, $$$$, 120
Mr. Beef, RN, $, 97
Murphy's, LV, $, 42
Mustard's Last Stand, EV, $, 8
Nookie, OT, $
Northside Bar & Grill, BWP, $$, 71
Orange, LV, $, 42
Original Hoagie Hut, LP, $, 58

Pane Bread Café, LV, $, 42
Perry's, LO, $, 111
Petterino's, LO, $$$, 108
Piece, BWP, $$, 70
Pops for Champagne, LV, $$$, 42
R.J. Grunts, LP, $$, 59
Red Lion, LP, $, 58
Rhapsody, LO, $$$, 109
Rivers, LO, $$$, 110
Rockit Bar & Grill, RN, $$$, 103
Rollin To Go, EV, $, 8
Roy's, GC, $$$, 124
Rumba, LO, $$$$, 117
Salt and Pepper Diner, LV, $, 40
Service Entrance, GC, $$, 123
Signature Room, GC, $$$$, 122
Simply Soup, LP, $, 59
South Water Kitchen, LO, $$$, 110
Spoon, OT, $$, 84
Stanley's Kitchen and Tap, OT, $$, 85
Sweet Thang, BWP, $, 70
Taste of Heaven, LV, $, 41
Tavern on Rush, GC, $$$$, 128
Tempo, GC, $$, 123
The Grillroom Chophouse and Wine Bar, LO $$, 115

136 Index

$ = less than $8
$$ = $8-$15
$$$ = $15-$25
$$$$ = $25+

unzipped.

Smoke Daddy, BWP, $$$, 72
Twin Anchors & Tavern, OT, $$, 89
Uncommon Ground, LV, $$, 43
Weber Grill, GC, $$$, 122
Weiner's Circle, LP, $$, 58
Windy City Wraps, GC, $, 121
Zig Zag, LP, $$, 58

Asian
Amarit, GC, $$, 123
Annam Café, EV, $$, 9
Big Bowl, GC, $$, 120
Blue Fin, BWP, $$, 73
Cafe Sushi, OT, $$, 84
Duck Walk, EV, $, 42
Green Ginger, BWP, $$, 72
Hama Matsu, EV, $$, 41
Hon Kee, UP, $$, 32
Koi, EV, $$, 8
Le Colonial, GC, $$$, 123
Matsu Yamma, LV, $$, 42
Sashimi Sashimi, EV, $, 8
Shine/Morida Rest., LP, $$, 57
Sun Wah Bar-B-Q Rest., UP, $, 32
Thai Pastry, UP, $, 32
To Pho Cafe, LO, $$, 109
Tsunami, GC, $$$, 120
Urban Tea Lounge, UP, $, 33
Vong's Thai Kitchen, RN, $$$, 96

Café
Albert's Café & Patisserie, GC, $$, 124
Argo Tea, LP, $, 59
Artist's Café, LO, $$, 117
Café Descartes, RP, $, 18
Café Express, EV, $, 10
F212, RN, $, 98
Filter, BWP, $, 70
Fresh Choice, OT, $, 85
Gallery Café, BWP, $, 79
Got Pizza Music Cafe, LO, $$, 117
Half and Half, BWP, $, 71
Harrison Snack Shop, LO, $, 112
Iguana Café, RN, $, 98
Jubilee Juice, LO, $, 117
Kafein, EV, $, 10
Kaffeccino, RP, $, 17
Metropolis Coffee Co., UP, $, 33
Panini Panini, RP, $, 16
Pick Me Up Café, LV, $, 40
The No Exit Café, UP, $, 32

European
Ann Sather, LV, $$, 40
The Berghoff, LO, $$$, 108
Brasserie Jo, RN, $$$, 97
Cullen's Bar and Grille, LV, $$, 40

Cyrano's Bistrot, Wine Bar & Cabaret, RN, $$, 98
La Creperie, LV, $, 43
La Fette, OT, $$$, 84
Noodles in the Pot, LP, $, 59
Swedish Bakery, UP, $$, 35

Sweet Stuff
Annette's Homemade Italian Ice, LP, $, 56
Anthony's Homemade Italian Ice, EV, $, 43
Australian Homemade, LV, $, 43
Bobtail Soda Fountain, LV, $, 44
Boulevard Treats, LO, $, 109
Fudge Pot, OT, $$, 85
Ghiradelli Soda Fountain & Chocolate Shop, GC, $, 126
The Hershey Co., GC, 127
Tin Tin, LP, $ 58

Italian
Buca di Beppo, GC, $$$, 124
Club Lucky, BWP, $$$, 73
Dave's Italian Kitchen, EV, $, 9
Harry Caray's, RN, $$$, 94
L8, RN, $$$, 97
Luciano's on Rush, GC, $$$, 123
Osteria Via Stato, RN, $$$$, 95
Pasta Palazzo, LP, $$, 57

Index 137

Phil Stefani's 437 Rush, GC, $$$, 124

Rosebud on Rush, GC, $$$, 122

The Italian Village, LO, $$$, 108

Trattoria No. 10, LO, $$$, 111

Tufano's Vernon Park Tap, LO, $$, 110

Venice Café, LO, $, 111

Mexican

Adobe Grill, OT, $$, 84

Burrito Beach, GC, $, 120

Chilpancingo, RN, $$$, 94

El Burrito Mexicano, EV, $, 41

El Gusto Taqueria Y Restaurante, BWP, $$, 70

El Jardin, EV, $$, 42

Emilio's Tapas Sol Y Nieve, GC, $$, 121

Fogo De Chao, RN, $$$$, 97

Frontera Grill/Topolobampo, RN, $$$, 94

La Baguette, LV, $, 44

Mambo Grill, RN, $$, 94

Nacional 27, RN, $$$, 98

Picante Taqueria, BWP, $$, 72

Tapas Barcelona, EV, $$, 8

Twisted Lizard, LP, $$, 56

Middle Eastern

Ayra Bhavan, RP, $$, 16

Babylon, BWP, $, 71

Café Suron, RP, $$, 17

Samah, LV, $$$, 44

Souk, BWP, $$$, 73

Tizi Melloul, RN, $$$, 96

Seafood

Blue Water Grill, RN, $$$, 94

Catch 35, LO, $$$, 110

Davis St. Fish Market, EV, $$$, 8

Sushi Samba, RN, $$$, 95

to bar hop.

Bar Louie, EV, 11

Big Chicks, UP, 36

Big Horse, EV, 78

Billy Goat Tavern, GC, 125

Blue Chicago, GC, 130

Borderline Tap, BWP, 78

Boss Bar, RN, 102

Bucktown Pub, BWP, 80

Burton Place, OT, 89

Cactus, GC, 129

Can's Bar, BWP, 79

Carol's Pub, UP, 37

City Pool Hall, RN, 102

Coyote Ugly, RN, 103

Cubby Bear, LV, 52

Elbo Room, LV, 53

Estelle's, BWP, 80

Exit, BWP, 80

Fado Irish Pub, RN, 97

Floyd's Pub, BWP, 78

Frankie Js, UP, 36

Gallery Cabaret, BWP, 79

Green Door Tavern, RN, 103

Green Mill, UP, 36

Hard Drive, LO, 116

Hi-Tops, LV, 53

Hogs and Honeys, OT, 88

Howl at the Moon, RN, 102

Hunt Club, GC, 129

Iggy's, BWP, 80

Jilly's Piano Bar, GC, 130

Joe's Sports Bar, OT, 89

Kit Kat Lounge, LV, 53

Lottie's, BWP, 79

Manhattan's, LO, 116

Nevins Pub, EV, 11

Nick's Beer Garden, BWP, 78

North Beach Chicago, OT, 88

O'Callaghans, RN,

O'Leary's Public House, RN, 104

Park West, LP, 66

Pepper Lounge, LV, 53

Pint, BWP, 78

Reserve, RN, 103

Roadhouse, OT, 88

Rockit Bar & Grill, RN, $$$, 103

Sheffield's, LV, 52

Spy Bar, LO, 116

Subterranean, BWP, 80

Sugar: A Dessert Bar, RN, 104

The Back Room, GC, 129

The Bar at The Peninsula, GC, 129

The Living Room in The W Hotel City Center, LO, 116

The Note, BWP, 78

The Underground Wonder Bar, GC, 130

Uptown Lounge, UP, 36

Wise Fool's Pub, LP, 66

Whiskey Sky, GC, 130

Zebra Lounge, GC, 130

138 Index

to club

Berlin, LV, 52

Blu, LP, 67

Cherry Red, LV, 52

Exit, RN, 104

Funky Buddha Lounge, RN, 104

Le Passage, GC, 131

Neo's, BWP, 80

Rednofive, RN, 104

Sound-Bar, RN, 105

Spin, LV, 53

SYN, GC, 131

Y, RN, 105

Zentra, OT, 89

to shop

2nd Hand Tunes, EV, 13

Accents Plus, EV, 13

All She Wrote, LP, 63

Al-Mansoor Video, RP, 10

Ancient Echoes, LP, 61

Another Time Another Place, EV, 12

Antiques on Michigan, LO, 112

Apartment #9, BWP, 75

Architectural Revolution, LV, 48

Armadillo's Pillow, RP, 22

Artcetera, UP, 35

Art Effect, LP, 61

Batteries Not Included, LV, 47

Beadazzled, EV, 12

Beatnix, LV, 48

Belmont Army/Navy Surplus, LV, 46

Blossom Flowers & Gifts, RP, 21

Bookworks, LV, 48

Broadway Antiques, LV, 49

Brown Elephant, BWP, 76

Buy Popular Demand, LP, 60

Caribbean American Baking Co., RP, 23

Chicago Costume Co., LP, 60

Clothes Optional, LV, 47

Cottage Jewelery, EV, 13

Council Thrift Shop, EV, 12

Cynthia Rowley, LP, 62

Daffodil Hill, BWP, 74

Disgraceland, LV, 50

Doolin's, RN, 99

Early to Bed, LV, 51

Elias, LV, 49

Equinox, RN, 99

Eurotrash, BWP, 76

Fischers Flowers, LP, 62

Flatts & Sharpe's Music Co., RP, 21

G Boutiques, BWP, 77

Garrett Popcorn Shop, LO, 122

Gaymart, LV, 47

Gramaphone, LV, 47

Hollywood Mirror, LV, 46

Hot Pink, BWP, 74

Hubba Hubba, LV, 49

Jane Hamill, LP, 63

Jive Monkey, LV, 51

Land of the Lost, LV, 47

Lost Eras, RP, 24

LuLu's at the Belle Kay, LV, 50

Lush, LP, 63

M. Boutique, LP, 63

McShane's Exchange, LP, 62

Medusa's Circle, LV, 46

Metal Haven, LV, 49

Mi Sun, LP, 63

Mrs. Catwalk, BWP, 77

My Masala, LP, 62

Myopic Books, BWP, 75

Newleaf Natural Grocery, RP, 20

Niche Footwear, BWP, 74

Nina, BWP, 79

Noir, BWP, 77

Nordstrom Rack, LO, 112

NYLA, GC, 126

Odd Obsession Movies, LP, 60

Old Town Aquarium, OT, 86

Orange Skin, BWP, 76

Original Expressions, LP, 61

Out of the West, LP, 60

Panache, LV, 50

Paper Source, LP, 61

Patel Brothers, RP, 20

Possibilities, EV, 12

PS: Accessories, GC, 126

PUMA Store Chicago, GC, 126

Quimby's, BWP, 74

Ragstock, LV, 47

Raizy D'Etre, BWP, 77

Reckless Records, BWP, 76

Recycle Men's and Women's Wear, BWP, 75

Resham's, RP, 22

Sage, LP, 62

Sara.Jane, OT, 86

Secret Treasures Antiques, EV, 12

Index 139

Shake Rattle and Read, UP, 35
Shane, LV, 48
Shred Shop, BWP, 77
Silver Moon, LV, 48
Sona Chandi, RP, 22
Sound Gallery, BWP, 76
String A Strand on Wells, OT, 86
Sukhadia's Sweets & Snacks, RP, 21
T-Shirt Deli, BWP, 74
Taboo Tabou, LV, 51
Tails in the City, GC, 127
Tattoo Factory, UP, 34
The Alley, LV, 46
The Mexican Shop, LV, 13
The Spice House, OT, 86
Tragically Hip, LV, 51
Tribeca, LP, 60
U S #1, BWP, 76
Una Mae's Freak Boutique, BWP, 75
Unan Imports, RP, 20
Uncle Fun, LV, 46
Under The Table Books, RP, 23
Untitled, BWP, 75
Up Down Tobacco, OT, 87
Vintage Deluxe, LV, 50
Viva Vintage, LV, 13
Windward Sports, LV, 50
Wooden Spoon, LV, 49
Yellow Jacket, LV, 51
"Z" Wallis Army Navy Depot, UP, 34

to watch.

Aragon Ballroom, UP, 36
Beat Kitchen, LP, 66
Double Door, BWP, 81
Gene Siskel Film Center, LO, 114
House of Blues, RN, 104
Riviera Theatre, UP, 27
Second City, OT, 88
Side Project, RP, 26
Symphony Center, LO, 114
Underground Lounge, LV, 52
Village North Theatre, RP

to try something else

10 Pin Bowling Lounge, RN, 102
Ame, LP, 61
American Male, RN, 99
Astrology Readings by Sara, GC, 128
Bank One Plaza, LO, 110
Body Chemistry, LV, 11
Chalet Wine and Cheese, GC, 127
Chicago Cultural Center, LO, 114
Chicago Public Library/ Harold Washington Library Center, LO, 114
Dave's Down to Earth Rock Shop and Prehistoric Life Museum, LV, 11
Dilshad's Hair Design, RP, 26
ESPN Zone, RN, 102
Lincoln Park Zoo, LP, 64
Loyola Park, RP, 26
Merlot on Maple, GC, 124
Millennium Park, LO, 113
Minute Massage, LO, 114

Museum of Contemporary Art: First Fridays, GC, 128
Navy Pier, GC, 128
Old Town Gardens, OT, 87
Puerto Vallarta, RN, 103
Potash Bros. Supermarket, GC, 127
Sweet Music Studio, RP, 27
Warren Park, RP, 26
Wrigley Field, LV, 45

to thank.

inspire, believe, appreciate, understand, help, vision, wonder, watch

Ben

Murphy Society
William White
Northwestern University
Majid Boroujerdi
Beth Abbott and Cathryn Timmers
Jeff Coney & Mary Kelly
Steve and Stuart from the Board of Directors
Vani and Julie (you are the best ever)
Brian Peters
Father Salmi and Loyola University
Al Attardo & WestCan Printing Group
Greg Stepanek from the CTA
Sylvie and my parents,
The city of Chicago.

Julie

Thank you to everyone who ever endured my persistent banter about this publication, as well as any person that had any sort of involvement: you guys made this vision possible. A great big thank you to Ben (and good luck!) and Vani for their endless hard work. Finally, my parents and my home, the wonderful city of Chicago.

Vani

Mumsie and Dad,
AnnaBanannaHead,
Julie (for rockin),
Benji (for being a dork),
Neel (for putting up with Crankypants),
Bosco (for taking me shopping),
'Maa' and 'Papa',
Ann Arbor Uncle and Auntie,
Forbes, O'brien & Novak from GBN,
Everyone else I drove crazy,
Bubble Tea
and Chicago.

Kim

Ben, Julie, Vani, and all the writers, designers and marketers for creating from scratch a fantastic book that will make a HUGE mark on the industry. It took so many months to put this together and couldn't have been done alone. Thanks for a great year, a great book and great company.

Sara

Bill Savage for cheeseburgers after the bike tour and everything else above and beyond a standard class. Brett for your phenomenal patience that stretches from the Hancock to the Sears Tower, even in 90 degree weather.

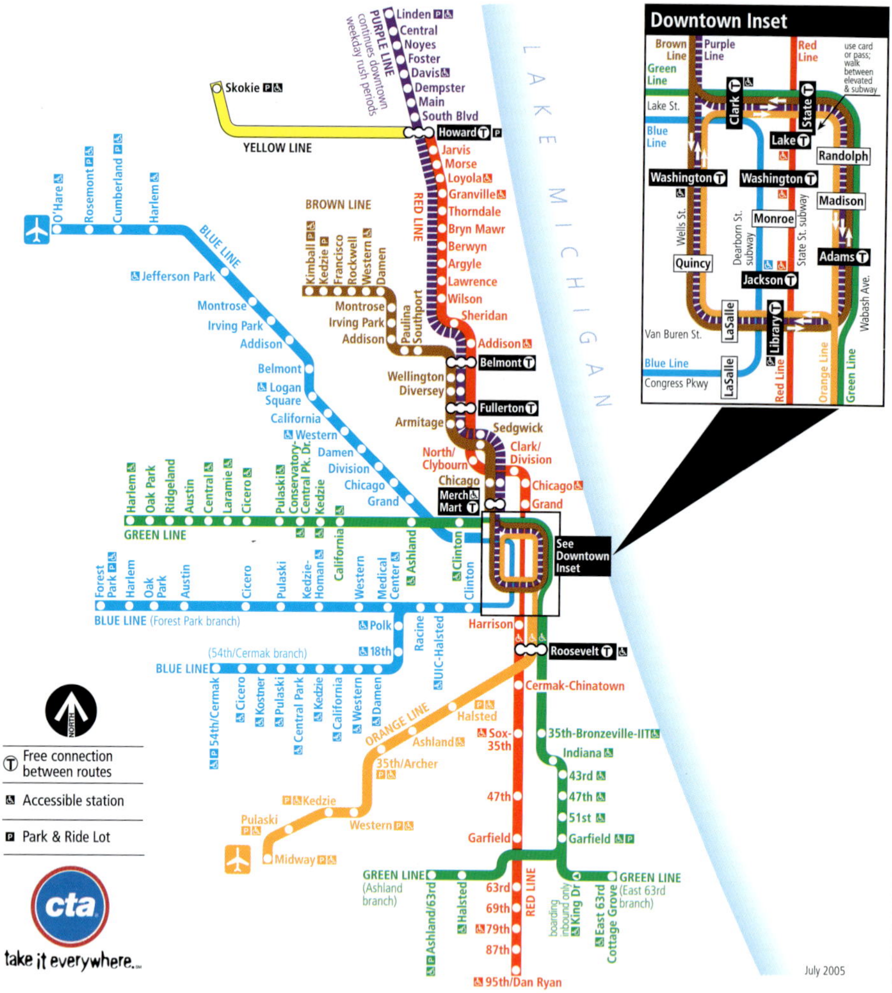

Downtown Inset
Brown Line
Purple Line
Green Line
Red Line
use card or pass; walk between elevated & subway
Lake St.
Blue Line
Clark
State
Lake
Randolph
Washington
Washington
Madison
Wells St.
Dearborn St. subway
State St. subway
Monroe
Quincy
Adams
Jackson
Wabash Ave.
LaSalle
Library
Van Buren St.
Blue Line
Congress Pkwy
LaSalle
Red Line
Orange Line
Green Line
LAKE MICHIGAN
PURPLE LINE continues downtown weekday rush periods
Linden
Central
Noyes
Foster
Davis
Dempster
Main
South Blvd
Howard
Skokie
YELLOW LINE
RED LINE
Jarvis
Morse
Loyola
Granville
Thorndale
Bryn Mawr
Berwyn
Argyle
Lawrence
Wilson
Sheridan
Addison
Belmont
Fullerton
Sedgwick
Clark/Division
Chicago
Grand
BROWN LINE
Kimball
Kedzie
Francisco
Rockwell
Western
Damen
Montrose
Irving Park
Addison
Paulina
Southport
Wellington
Diversey
Armitage
North/Clybourn
Chicago
Merch Mart
O'Hare
Rosemont
Cumberland
Harlem
BLUE LINE
Jefferson Park
Montrose
Irving Park
Addison
Belmont
Logan Square
California
Western
Damen
Division
Chicago
Grand
Harlem
Oak Park
Ridgeland
Austin
Central
Laramie
Cicero
Pulaski
Conservatory-Central Pk. Dr.
Kedzie
California
Ashland
Clinton
GREEN LINE
Forest Park
Harlem
Oak Park
Austin
Cicero
Pulaski
Kedzie-Homan
California
Western
Medical Center
Racine
Clinton
UIC-Halsted
BLUE LINE (Forest Park branch)
Polk
18th
(54th/Cermak branch)
BLUE LINE
54th/Cermak
Cicero
Kostner
Pulaski
Central Park
Kedzie
California
Western
Damen
See Downtown Inset
Harrison
Roosevelt
Cermak-Chinatown
ORANGE LINE
Halsted
Ashland
35th/Archer
Kedzie
Pulaski
Western
Midway
Sox-35th
47th
Garfield
35th-Bronzeville-IIT
Indiana
43rd
47th
51st
Garfield
GREEN LINE (Ashland branch)
Ashland/63rd
Halsted
63rd
69th
79th
87th
95th/Dan Ryan
RED LINE
boarding inbound only
King Dr
East 63rd
Cottage Grove
GREEN LINE (East 63rd branch)
NORTH
Free connection between routes
Accessible station
Park & Ride Lot
take it everywhere.

July 2005